PIAGET'S THEORY OF
COGNITIVE DEVELOPMENT

PIAGET'S THEORY OF
COGNITIVE DEVELOPMENT
An Introduction
for Students of Psychology and Education

Second Edition

BARRY J. WADSWORTH
Mount Holyoke College

WITH DRAWINGS BY THE AUTHOR

LONGMAN
NEW YORK AND LONDON

PIAGET'S THEORY OF COGNITIVE DEVELOPMENT
An Introduction for Students of Psychology and Education

Second Edition

Longman Inc., New York
Associated companies, branches, and representatives
throughout the world.

Developmental Editor: Nicole Benevento
Editorial and Design Supervisor: Linda Salmonson
Design: Angela Foote
Manufacturing and Production Supervisor: Louis Gaber
Composition: A & S Graphics, Inc.
Printing and Binding: The Murray Printing Company

Library of Congress Cataloging in Publication Data

Wadsworth, Barry J
    Piaget's theory of cognitive development.

        Bibliography: p.
        Includes index.
        1. Piaget, Jean, 1896-   2. Cognition in children
I. Title. [DNLM: 1. Child psychology.
2. Cognition—In infancy and childhood. WS105.5.C7
W124p]
BF723.C5W33 1979   155.4'13   79-12347
ISBN 0-582-28124-5

Manufactured in the United States of America

J   I   H   G   F   E   D   C   B   A
8   7   6   5   4   3   2   1   0   9

Preface to the First Edition

The purpose of this book, as envisioned by the author, is to introduce the education or psychology undergraduate student to the basic concepts of Jean Piaget's theory of cognitive development. The writings of Piaget are extremely relevant to both education and psychology, but to the student not familiar with Piaget's concepts and vocabulary, reading his works is a monumental task. Most of Piaget's writings were first published in French and have undergone translation into English. In addition, a complete understanding of some of Piaget's works cannot be obtained without some sophistication in mathematics, epistemology, and logic.

Jean Flavell's invaluable book *The Developmental Psychology of Jean Piaget* (1963) ties together the multitude of writings by Piaget and his associates. It is a reference that can take the reader quickly and accurately to the essential points of Piaget's system. But, because Flavell's book is itself of necessity very sophisticated, it usually cannot be read with ease the first time around by students. To the writer it seems an overall picture of Piaget's system is necessary before the particulars can be appreciated.

The writer has attempted to present Piaget's major concepts and notions in a simplified, conceptual manner in the hope that such an initiation to Piagetian concepts and vocabulary will be adequate to allow the reader to pursue with greater initial facility Piaget's own works and the research his writings have generated. Such an approach runs the risk of some distortion and incompleteness. This book does not cover all Piaget has to say. The emphasis has been placed on cognitive development as it relates to education and learning.

It is hoped that those reading this work will find Piaget's concepts (as construed by the writer) fascinating and appealing enough to go on to Piaget's own words where the real fruits are to be had.

Preface to the Second Edition

Eight years ago, the first edition of *Piaget's Theory of Cognitive Development* was published. In the early 1970s Piaget's concepts of the development of children's thinking, reasoning, and intellectual skills were gaining some popularity with psychologists and educators in the United States. Now Piaget's concepts are at the center of psychological thought, and there is no evidence that interest in his theory is decreasing.[1]

In the recent history of education, no psychological theory relevant to education has advanced to the fore with such appeal to educators, and with so much research support, as Piagetian theory. It is therefore amazing that so little of Piaget's theory has been incorporated into educational practice. A look at the schools reveals little influence of developmental theory on the thinking and practices of educators. What influence there has been exists largely at pre-school and kindergarten levels. The forces that move education practice are rooted in tradition and politics; they mold the schools with no regard for the increasing knowledge available about children's development. Certainly elements of traditional education should be preserved. What we must address is whether they should be preserved for their own sake or because rational educational and social reasons exist for preserving them.

American education is currently involved in a "back to basics"

[1] A study of the frequency of citation in *Child Development* for 1974 finds 22 authors referenced 10 or more times. The most frequently referenced authors were Jean Piaget (89 references), John Flavell (45), Barbel Inhelder (Piaget's co-worker, 45), Jerome Kagan (38), and Robert Fantz (23).

movement. Unfortunately, back to basics usually means going back to the way we were doing things before. This does not necessarily result in educational improvement.

The 1960s saw the introduction of new curriculum concepts and materials in the public schools. One example is the "new math," which Piaget's name became associated with. The new math was a flop and resulted in a lot of frustrated children, teachers, and parents. Certainly, people who have not understood what Piaget has been trying to say may suspect that because his theory was used by some to lend credence to the new math approach, the failure of the new math is also a failure of Piagetian theory. This is not the case. The new math failed because it did not really consider the way children acquire mathematical knowledge, and because the methods of teaching it were no different from the methods of teaching the "old math." Piagetians would have predicted the result.

Piaget's theory does not deserve to be associated with the poor results of the new math. Piaget has told us that to understand children, we must study children. We cannot appreciate children's methods of learning merely by reflecting on, or reading about, them from an adult perspective. We must work with and study children.

Piagetian theory has not changed much during the past ten years, but some of the educational interpretations of Piaget's work have changed substantially and have generally become more sophisticated. Ten years ago, interpreters of Piagetian theory found little support in the theory for the belief that schooling could significantly aid children's acquisition of *knowledge.* Today the interpretations tend to be much more positive about the potential effect of schooling on children.

With this in mind, I decided to revise *Piaget's Theory of Cognitive Development.* I continue to receive encouraging comments about the book from teachers and students and am pleased that readers find it readable and understandable. In this revised edition I have tried to preserve the readability of the first edition while updating and expanding the book's content. The major addition to the text is a chapter on Piaget's work on *moral judgment.*

There has been some criticism that the original book is incomplete and unsophisticated, and does not adequately cover Piagetian research. Both editions of this book are meant to be *introductions* to Piaget's theory and no more. Neither covers all of Piaget's work nor claims to evaluate all the relevant research. My goals have been to present Piaget's theory in a clear and concise manner. I hope my readers will find this new edition a readable and thought-provoking introduction to Piaget's theory.

To Barn at his first birthday,
Eva who has helped us both,
and my mother and father

Acknowledgments

The author wishes to thank the following publishers for their kind permission to reprint:

Basic Books from *The Construction of Reality in the Child* by Jean Piaget, translated by Margaret Cook, © 1954 by Basic Books, Inc., Publishers, New York; *The Growth of Logical Thinking from Childhood to Adolescence* by Barbel Inhelder and Jean Piaget, translated by Stanley Milfram, 1958; *The Psychology of the Child* by Jean Piaget and Barbel Inhelder, translated from the French by Helen Weaver, 1969.

Free Press from *The Moral Judgment of the Child* by Jean Piaget, © 1965 by Free Press.

Humanities Press from *Language and Thought of the Child* by Jean Piaget, 1959; *The Child's Conception of Space* by Jean Piaget and Barbel Inhelder, 1948; *Judgment and Reasoning in the Child* by Jean Piaget, 1928.

International Universities Press, Inc., from *The Origins of Intelligence in Children* by Jean Piaget, © 1953 by International Universities Press, Inc.

Random House, Inc., from *Six Psychological Studies* by Jean Piaget, edited by David Elkind, 1968. © 1967 by Random House, Inc.

Routledge and Kegan Paul Ltd. from *Language and Thought of the Child* by Jean Piaget, 1926; *Judgment and Reasoning in the Child* by Jean Piaget, 1926; *The Child's Construction of Reality* by Jean Piaget, 1955; *The Growth of Logical Thinking: From Childhood to Adolescence* by Jean Piaget and Barbel Inhelder, 1958; *The Child's Conception of Space* by Jean Piaget and Barbel Inhelder, 1967.

The Society for Research in Child Development, Inc. from Lawrence Kohlberg, "Early Education: A Cognitive-Developmental View," *Child Development*, 39 (1969).

Van Nostrand Reinhold Company from *The Developmental Psychology of Jean Piaget* by John H. Flavell, 1963, Copyright © 1963 by Litton Educational Publishing, Inc.

Contents

List of Tables

PIAGET'S THEORY OF
COGNITIVE DEVELOPMENT

If the child partly explains the adult, it can be said that each period of his development partly explains the periods that follow.

Piaget and Inhelder, 1969, p. 3

Introduction

Jean Piaget's college and university training was in the natural sciences. His main interests originally were in biology. Early in his career he became interested in children's intellectual development, and has spent the last sixty years gathering an impressive amount of research information pertaining to mental development. His work has produced an elaborate and comprehensive theory of how intelligence develops.[1] Piaget has functioned as a biologist, philosopher, logician, psychologist, and educator. In each of these fields he has made original contributions, though his contributions have had their greatest impact on psychology and education.

Piaget is thought of primarily as a child psychologist and educator in America. In the strict sense of the word, he is neither. His work is not directly concerned with predicting behavior as the psychologist's frequently is, nor is he directly concerned with how to teach children. He prefers to be classified as a genetic epistemologist.[2] His work is primarily concerned with describing and explaining in a very

---

[1] In this writing, the terms *intellectual, cognitive,* and *mental* will be used interchangeably.

[2] Genetic epistemology is a science of how knowledge is acquired.

systematic way the growth and development of intellectual structures and knowledge. Needless to say, his work has had a great impact on both education and psychology here and abroad.

Piaget's publications, all written originally in French, took many years to cross the Atlantic. Only recently have Piaget's works and concepts been spreading quickly throughout educational and psychological thought in America. L'Abate's 1968 frequency of citation study[3] is a measure of the impact of Piaget's works on American thought. His search of journals and textbooks in the child development field during the 1950s and 1960s found Piaget to be the most frequently cited author.

BIOGRAPHY

Piaget's life has been one of scholarship and hard work. He was born in 1896 in Neuchâtel, Switzerland. By his own admission, he was an intellectually precocious youth. At the age of 10, he managed his first publication, a description of a partly albino sparrow he observed in a public park. To some extent, the direction and rigor of Piaget's efforts were determined early in his life. At the age of 15, he had decided to direct his work toward a biological explanation of knowledge, a goal that is still clearly reflected in his work.

In 1915, at the age of 18, Piaget received his baccalaureate from the University of Neuchâtel in Switzerland. Three years later, he received a doctorate in the natural sciences from the same school. During this period, much of Piaget's time was spent studying the development of mollusks in the many lakes around Neuchâtel. By the age of 21, he had

---

[3] Two journals, *Child Development* (1950-1965) and *Journal of Genetic Psychology* (1957-1958, 1960-1965) were searched, along with twelve popular and current textbooks on child development.

published twenty-five professional papers (mostly on mollusks), and was considered one of the world's few experts on mollusks.

His intensive work in biology led him to conclude that biological development was due not only to maturation (and heredity) but also to variables in the environment. He observed in successive generations of mollusks certain structural changes that could only be attributed to movement from large lakes with much wave action to small ponds. Such observations convinced Piaget that biological development was a process of adaptation to the environment; that it could not be explained by maturation alone (Piaget, "Autobiography," 1952, p. 250). Experiences and convictions such as these contributed to Piaget's later view of mental development as being primarily a process of adaptation to the environment and an extension of biological development.[4]

After completing his doctorate, Piaget's primary interest turned to psychology. For several years he had been reading books on and taking classes in psychology, and he had become increasingly interested in the field. He went to Zurich in 1918 and studied and worked in several psychological clinics, deciding to immerse himself in psychological experimentation. In 1919 he went to Paris and spent two years at the Sorbonne. While in Paris, Piaget had a chance to work in Binet's[4] laboratory (a grade school) standardizing several tests. Unenthusiastic at first, he became intrigued with the incorrect answers children gave to questions on the tests, and shortly thereafter, he was hard at work examining the reasoning processes underlying

---

[4] Mental development as a form of adaptation in the biological sense, one of Piaget's revolutionary and most important concepts, is developed in Chapter One.

[5] Binet is considered father of the Binet Intelligence Test from which the current forms of the Stanford-Binet were derived.

children's responses. Piaget had found his research interest. For two years he continued testing children, examining the development of their thought. This was the beginning of Piaget's experimental activity in psychology.

In 1921 Piaget was offered the position of director of studies at the Institut J. J. Rousseau in Geneva (Ibid., p. 245), a position that proved to be the perfect environment for the studies he was interested in. He accepted the position and was launched on a course of research that has not changed since: the investigation of the mental development of children.

By the age of 30, Piaget was famous for his initial works in psychology.[6] Through the years he has conducted a continuous research, and he has taught at the University of Geneva. A prolific writer, he has published over thirty books and hundreds of journal articles, several in conjunction with the colleagues he has assembled in Geneva. He attributes much of his own productivity to the group of co-workers that have worked with him over the years.

Piaget is reported to be an untiring worker, at 83 still following a strenuous daily self-imposed work schedule. Each summer, at the school year's end, he is reported (Elkind, 1968) to collect his research findings for the year and head for an abandoned farmhouse in the Alps where he spends the summer in isolation, writing and walking, his whereabouts unknown to but a few friends and his family. When the summer ends, Piaget returns from the mountains—with a new book or two—and several articles (Elkind, 1968).

Piaget has been honored around the world. He holds

---

[6] *The Language and Thought of the Child* (1924) and *Judgment and Reasoning of the Child* (1924) were Piaget's first books published in psychology, though he had published numerous papers in the field prior to these publications.

honorary degrees from Harvard (1936), Columbia (1970), the University of Brussels (1949), the Sorbonne (1946), and Brazil (1949). In recent years he has made several trips to the United States to address American groups concerned with child development.

In 1955, with the help of a grant from the Rockefeller Foundation, the Centre International d'Epistémologie Génétique was established in Geneva. This program permits three eminent scholars a year to visit and do research with the Geneva group that has grown up around Piaget. Several Americans have studied in Geneva under this program, and to some extent, this has helped spread interest in Piaget's work. Whether Piaget's efforts and basic assumptions prove to be correct or incorrect in total or in part, his works have generated more interest and research than those of any other person in psychology in the last fifty years.

APPROACH TO RESEARCH

Piaget is a developmental psychologist in that he is concerned with uncovering the ontogenetic[7] changes in cognitive functioning from birth through adolescence. His works have been slow to gain wide attention in the United States. The reasons for this (aside from the already-mentioned fact that his works were all originally published in French) are many, but in large part these reasons are theoretical and methodological. The concepts he uses have not gained acceptance easily in the United States, nor has his "experimental" methodology.

Psychology in the United States has a strong tradition of behaviorism. Such men as Thorndike, Tolman, Watson,

---

[7] Ontogenetic: those developmental changes that occur in the individual.

Hull, Spence, and Skinner have dominated the scene, each of them primarily interested in stimulus-response relationships and the concept of reinforcement. Traditionally, American psychologists of the behaviorist school do not infer the existence of internal mental processes (of thought). Piaget's concepts like assimilation are entirely foreign to the behaviorist position. He does not conceptualize behavior in terms of stimuli and responses, nor does he use the construct of reinforcement. Some of Piaget's important concepts are assimilation, accommodation, equilibrium, and schemata. Also, he does infer the existence of internal mental processes. Consequently, it has been difficult for American psychologists to come to grips with Piaget's concepts.

In America, experimental research in psychology has typically concerned itself with hypothesis testing, rigorous control of experimental variables, and treatment of data with sophisticated statistical procedures. Most of Piaget's research has not been experimental, nor does he frequently employ elaborate statistics and test hypotheses. From his work in Paris in Binet's clinic, Piaget evolved a clinical-descriptive technique that came to serve as a trademark for his work. It essentially involved asking individual children carefully selected questions and noting their responses. In other cases, data were nothing more than the observation of infant behavior. These techniques could hardly be called experimental in the restricted sense of the word (they are basically observational), though they were invariably systematic and his analyses were exceedingly detailed: designed to detect developmental changes in cognitive functioning.

Piaget frequently permitted himself to be led by his "intuition" when interviewing children, particularly in his earlier works. In the clinical approach, any two children are not necessarily asked the same questions in the same setting. In effect, no two children ever receive the same experimental treatment. *The Child's Conception of the World* (1929) is an example of Piaget's skillful selection of questions. The book is without statistical tables, and "sample sizes" are small. The main sources for two of Piaget's books were observations of his own three children, born between 1925 and 1931.[8] These meticulous observations provided him with an awareness of the relationship between early sensori-motor actions and later cognitive development. From these exceedingly complete and careful descriptions of behavior over a period of years, major conclusions have been drawn regarding intellectual development from birth to age 2. This type of research has been criticized severely by some because of the small "sample size," and because it is not experimental. The criticisms diminish in importance if one accepts the assumption implicit in Piaget's theory: that the general course of development of intellectual structures is the same in all persons. If this is true, then sample sizes can become meaningless.[9] It should also be stated that there is much merit in using the longitudinal approach that Piaget has used. While frequently observing small numbers of children, his observations of the same subjects have on occasion ranged over years.

While much of Piaget's early work can be looked upon as intuitive, employing nonexperimental procedures and using small samples of subjects, a large part of his more recent work is as rigorously experimental as any psychologist might wish. *The Early Growth of Logic in the Child* (1964) and *The Mechanisms of Perception* (1969) care-

---

[8] *Play, Dreams, and Imitation in Childhood* (1951), *The Origins of Intelligence in Children* (1952).

[9] Considerable evidence exists that the *course* of cognitive development is basically the same in *all* people, with some variation reflective of culture.

fully report statistical findings and respectable sample sizes. The material reported in *The Growth of Logical Thinking from Childhood to Adolescence* (1958) is based on the testing of over 1500 subjects.

While many criticisms have been leveled at Piaget's approach to research, none has disputed that it is always systematic, rigorous, and insightful. Piaget's primary technique has been one of systematic observation, description, and analysis of children's behavior. This approach is primarily designed to discover the nature and level of development of the concepts children use, not to produce developmental scales. Piaget defends the approach he has taken to research on the basis that it is the most appropriate for the questions he seeks to answer. While this is very reasonable, it does not always rest well with one who has sanctified American experimental procedures.

THE ORGANIZATION OF THE BOOK

One of the difficulties encountered by the uninitiated in reading Piaget's works is a number of unique concepts he uses to conceptualize behavior. It is necessary to understand these before his works can be understood. Chapter One is a description of four of the concepts that are central to all Piaget's work: schema, assimilation, accommodation, and equilibrium. Chapter Two deals with the relationship between cognitive development and factors such as heredity, action, motivation, and stages of development.

Each of Chapters Three through Six deals with one of the four stages of cognitive development, in the order in which they occur. Chapter Seven discusses the relationship of cognitive development to adolescent behavior. The final chapter summarizes the previous chapters and discusses some of the implications of Piaget's works for child training and education.

Chapter One

Intellectual Organization and Adaptation

Piaget's system for conceptualizing cognitive development has been greatly influenced by his early training and work as a biologist. Functioning as a biologist, he became vividly aware of and impressed by the interaction of mollusks with their environment. Mollusks, like all living organisms, are constantly adapting to changes in environmental conditions.

From this early work, Piaget came to believe that biological acts are acts of *adaptation* to the physical environment and *organizations* of the environment. This led him to conceptualize intellectual development in much the same way. Cognitive acts are seen as acts of *organization* of and *adaptation* to the perceived environment. This is not to imply in any sense that mental behavior can be attributed to biological functioning, but that the concepts of biological development are useful and valid for looking at intellectual development. Indeed, Piaget asserts (*The Origins of Intelligence in Children*, 1952) that the basic principles of cognitive development are the *same* as those of biological development.

Organization and adaptation are not viewed by Piaget as separate processes. He writes:

> From the biological point of view organization is inseparable
> from adaptation: They are two complementary processes of a
> single mechanism, the first being the internal aspect of the
> cycle of which adaptation constitutes the external aspect
> [Piaget, Ibid., p. 7].

For Piaget, intellectual activity cannot be separated from
the "total" functioning of the organism. Thus, he considers intellectual functioning as a special form of biological
activity (Ibid., p. 42). Intellectual and biological activity
are both part of the overall process by which an organism
adapts to the environment and organizes experience.

To understand the processes of intellectual organization
and adaptation as they are viewed by Piaget, four basic
concepts are required. These are the concepts of *schema,
assimilation, accommodation,* and *equilibrium.* These concepts are used to explain how and why mental development occurs. They are discussed in that order.

SCHEMA

Piaget believed the mind had to have structures much in
the same way the body does. All animals have a stomach, a
structure that permits eating and digestion. To help explain why children (all persons) make rather stable responses to stimuli, and to account for many of the phenomena associated with memory, Piaget used the word
schema. Schemata are the cognitive or mental *structures*
by which individuals intellectually adapt to and organize
the environment. *Schemata* are structures that are the
mental counterparts of biological means of adapting. The
stomach is a biological structure that animals use successfully to adapt to their environment. In much the same
way, schemata are equivalent structures that adapt and
change with mental development. These structures are in-

ferred to exist. They are constructs in the same way that Freud's Id and Ego are.[1]

They are constructs in the same way that Freud's Id and Ego are.

Schemata can be simplistically thought of as concepts or categories. Another analogy might be an index file in which each index card represents a schema. Adults have many cards or schemata. They are used to process and identify incoming stimuli. In this way the organism is able to differentiate between stimulus events and to generalize. When a child is born, it has few schemata (cards on file). As the child develops, his schemata gradually broaden (become more generalized), become more differentiated, and progressively more "adult." Schemata never stop changing or becoming more refined. Indeed, the sensori-motor schemata of childhood develop into the schemata of adulthood. So we have a picture of an index card file in the child's head. At birth it contains only a few large cards on which everything is written. As the child develops, more cards are necessary to contain the changing classifications. As an illustration, imagine a child walking down a country road with his parents. The child looks into a field and sees what is conventionally called a cow. The child says, "Look at the big dog!" What does the child's response mean in terms of intellectual functioning? Assuming the child made an honest response, we could infer something like this: The child looked out into the field and saw a cow. Presented with this "new" stimulus (he never saw a cow before), the child tried to place the stimulus in reference to a

---

[1] Constructs are concepts or "things" that are not directly observable but are inferred to exist (e.g., intelligence, creativity, aptitude, ability, motivation, instincts). The list of constructs can be endless. A main activity of psychological research is to try to clarify the nature of constructs.

card in his card file. In terms of the things the child could identify, the stimulus (cow) most closely approximated a dog, so the child identified the object as a dog (a schema or file).

In Piaget's terms, we would say that the child has a number of schemata. These schemata are analogous to concepts, categories, or cards in a file. When confronted with a stimulus, the child tried to "fit" the stimulus into an available schema. Thus the child quite logically called the cow a dog, since the cow closely approximated a dog, and met all the child's criteria for what a dog was. The child was not able to perceive the differences between a cow and a dog, but he was able to see the similarities.

Schemata are intellectual structures that organize events as they are perceived by the organism into groups according to common characteristics. They are repeatable psychological events in the sense that the child will repeatedly classify stimuli in a consistent manner. If the child "consistently" classifies cows as dogs, we can infer something about the nature of the child's concepts (schemata of cows and dogs).

At birth, schemata are reflexive in nature. That is, they can be inferred from simple reflex motor activities such as sucking and grasping. The sucking reflex illustrates a reflexive schema. At birth, infants typically will suck on whatever is put in their mouths—a nipple, a finger—suggesting that there is no differentiation, or that only a single, global sucking schema exists. Shortly after birth, infants learn to differentiate: milk-producing stimuli are accepted and non-milk-producing stimuli are rejected. At this point, a differentiation exists, or in Piaget's words, the infant has two sucking schemata, one for milk-producing stimuli and one for non-milk-producing stimuli. At this time, schemata are not yet "mental" in the sense in which we usually think of the term. Schemata are reflexive. The infant makes real differentiations within his limited environment, but they are made via the reflexive and motor apparatus he has available. These differentiations on the most primitive level are the precursors of later "mental" activities. As the child develops, schemata become more differentiated, less sensory, more numerous, and the network they form becomes increasingly more complex. During early childhood, an infant has a few reflexive schemata that allow him to make very few differentiations in the environment. An adult has a vast array of comparatively complex schemata that permit a great number of differentiations. The schemata of the adult evolve from the schemata of the child through adaptation and organization.

It would be misleading to think that schemata do not change, or that the child is destined to call cows dogs for the rest of his days. Obviously, this does not happen. As the child becomes better able to differentiate between stimuli, schemata become more numerous (differentiated). As he becomes better able to generalize across stimuli, schemata become more refined.

At any point in time, a child's responses are assumed to reflect the nature of the child's concepts or schemata at that time. It is entirely "logical" for the child described in the example to call a cow a dog when the schemata he has available are considered. Schemata are defined by (or reflected in) the overt behavior of the child. But schemata are more than the behavior; they are the internal structure from which the behaviors flow. Behavior patterns that occur repeatedly in the course of cognitive activity are conceptualized as reflecting schemata. A schema subsumes a whole collection of distinct but similar action sequences. "Every schema is . . . coordinated with all other schemata and itself constitutes a totality with differentiated parts" (Piaget, *The Origins of Intelligence in Children*, 1952, p.7).

Since schemata are structures of cognitive development that do change, allowance must be made for their growth and development. Adults have different concepts from children. Concepts (schemata—their structural counterparts) change. The cognitive schemata of the adult are derived from the sensori-motor schema of the child. The processes responsible for the change are *assimilation* and *accommodation*.

ASSIMILATION

Assimilation is the cognitive *process* by which the person integrates new perceptual matter or stimulus events into existing schemata or patterns of behavior. One might say that the child has experiences: It sees new things (cows) or sees old things in new ways, and hears things. What the child tries to do is to fit these new events or stimuli into the schemata he has at the time.[2] Suppose, as in the previous example, a child is walking down the country road with his father, and the father points to a cow in the field and says, "What is that?" The child looks at the cow (stimulus) and says, "That's a dog." What has happened? The child, seeing the object in the field (cow), sifted through his collection of schemata until he found one that seemed appropriate and that could include the object. To the child, the object (cow) had all the characteristics of a dog—it fit in his dog schema—so the child concluded that the object was a dog. The stimulus (cow) was assimilated into the dog schema. Thus assimilation can be viewed as the cognitive process of placing new stimulus events into existing schemata.

Assimilation goes on all the time. It would be extreme

---

[2] Assimilation is a term Piaget borrowed from biology. It is the cognitive counterpart of eating, wherein food is eaten, digested, and assimilated or changed into a usable form.

oversimplification to suggest that a person processes one stimulus at a time. The human must continually process an increasing number of stimuli.

Assimilation theoretically does not result in the development (change) of schemata, but does affect their growth.

One might compare a schema to a balloon, and assimilation to putting more air in the balloon. The balloon gets larger (assimilation growth) but does not change its shape (development). Assimilation is a part of the process by which the individual cognitively adapts to and organizes the environment. The process of assimilation allows for growth of schemata. This does not account for change (development) of schemata. We know schemata change— adult schemata are different from children's. Piaget accounts for the change of schemata with *accommodation.*

ACCOMMODATION

Upon being confronted with a new stimulus, the child tries to assimilate it into existing schemata. Sometimes this is not possible. Sometimes a stimulus cannot be placed or assimilated into a schema because there are no schemata into which it fits. The characteristics of the stimulus do not approximate those required in any of the child's available schemata. What does the child do? Essentially he can do one of two things: He can create a new schema into which he can place the stimulus, or he can modify an existing schema so that the stimulus will fit into it; both of these are forms of *accommodation*. Thus, accommodation is the creation of new schemata or the modification of old schemata. Both of these actions result in a change in or development of cognitive structures (schemata).

Once accommodation has taken place, the child can try again to assimilate the stimulus. Since the structure has changed, the stimulus is readily assimilated. Assimilation is always the end-product that the child actively seeks.

The child who is actively assimilating and accommodating is in no way required or expected to evolve schemata that assume a particular form. Implicit in the conceptualizations of schema used here is the idea that schemata develop over time with experience. At first, while the child is an infant, they are very global—and when compared to adults, extremely imprecise and frequently inaccurate. The processes of assimilation and accommodation that convert infants' rather primitive schemata into the more sophisticated adult-like schemata obviously take years.

Another word about assimilation and accommodation. It can be seen that in assimilation, the person imposes his available structure on the stimuli being processed. That is,

Sometimes you just have to accommodate!

the stimuli are "forced" to fit the person's structure. In accommodation, the reverse is true. The person is "forced" to change his schema to fit the new stimuli. Accommodation accounts for development (a qualitative change), and assimilation accounts for growth (a quantitative change); together they account for intellectual adaptation and the development of intellectual structures.

EQUILIBRIUM

The processes of assimilation and accommodation are necessary for cognitive growth and development. Of equal importance are the relative amounts of assimilation and accommodation that take place. For example, imagine the logical outcome in terms of mental development if a person always assimilated stimuli and never accommodated. Such a person would end up with a few very large schemata and be unable to detect differences in things. Most things would be seen as similar. On the other hand, what would be the result if the person always accommodated and never assimilated? This would result in a person having a great number of very small schemata that would have little generality. Most things would be seen as different. The person would be unable to detect similarities. Either of these extremes would be disastrous. Thus it can be seen that a "balance" between assimilation and accommodation is as necessary as the processes themselves. The "balance" between assimilation and accommodation is referred to by Piaget as *equilibrium*. It is necessary to ensure an efficient interaction of the developing child with the environment.

Equilibrium is a balance between assimilation and accommodation. *Disequilibrium* is an imbalance between assimilation and accommodation.[3] When disequilibrium occurs, cognitively, it provides motivation for the child to seek equilibrium—to further assimilate or accommodate. Equilibrium is seen as a necessary condition toward which the organism constantly strives. The organism ultimately assimilates all stimuli (or stimulus events) with or without accommodation. This results in equilibrium. Thus, equilibrium can be viewed as a state of cognitive "balance" that is reached at assimilation. Obviously, equilibrium relevant to any particular stimulus may be a very temporary affair, but it is nonetheless important.

Everything must be assimilated by the child. The schemata the child uses may not be in harmony with those of adults (like classifying a cow as a dog), but the child's organization will *always* be internally consistent. The child's placement of stimuli into schemata is theoretically always appropriate for his level of conceptual develop-

---

[3] Disequilibrium can be thought of as "cognitive conflict" resulting when expectations or predictions are not confirmed by experience. A child expects something to happen in a certain way and it does not. The discrepancy between the expected and what actually occurs is a form of disequilibrium.

| Where can I put this? | Ah . . . ha . . .! | Love that equilibrium! |

ment. There is no "wrong" placement. There are just better and better placements.

We can say, then, that the child, upon experiencing a new stimulus (or an old one again), tries to assimilate the stimulus into an existing schema. If he is successful, equilibrium is attained for the moment, relevant to the particular stimulus event. If the child cannot assimilate the stimulus, he then attempts to accommodate by modifying a schema or creating a new one. When this is done, assimilation of the stimulus proceeds and equilibrium is reached.

Conceptually, cognitive growth and development proceeds in this way at *all* levels of development, from birth through adulthood, the schemata of the adult being built from the schemata of the child. It is important to note that in assimilation, the organism "fits" stimuli into schemata that exist, while in accommodation the organism "changes" schemata to fit the stimulus. It can be seen that the process of accommodation results in a qualitative change in intellectual structures (schemata) while assimilation only adds to the existing structures—a quantitative change. Thus it is that assimilation and accommodation, a cumulative coordination and integration, account for the growth and development of cognitive structures.

Chapter Two

Cognitive Development and Other Factors

HEREDITY AND COGNITIVE DEVELOPMENT

Piaget (*The Origins of Intelligence in Children*, 1952) subscribes to the importance of heredity in all development, both biological and intellectual. He asserts that to some degree inherited neurological structures impede or facilitate intellectual functioning, but that they cannot account for intellectual functioning by themselves (Ibid., pp. 1-3). Inherited neurological structures influence cognitive development, but the structure alone cannot explain the development. Piaget asserts that properties other than neurological structures are inherited that affect cognitive development, in part account for individual differences, and make intellectual progress possible. These properties are called *functional invariants*.

The functional invariants are essentially the processes of assimilation and accommodation that permit cognitive organization and adaptation. These functional invariants can be thought of as combining to produce *a mode of intellectual functioning*—the particular way in which a particular organism adapts to and organizes the environment. An individual could be one who tends to assimilate more than he accommodates. Variations in the relative amounts of assimilation and accommodation can be thought of as a mode of functioning. The mode remains fixed (invariant) throughout the course of one's life, each individual having a unique, genetically determined mode. According to Piaget, in cognitive development, development that is environmentally, as well as genetically determined, biological endowment plays a role, but *does not* predetermine intellectual functioning at any given point in life. The functioning and structures that develop after birth are determined by the interaction of the inherited properties and the environment (experience). Thus neither experience alone nor endowment alone can determine cognitive development.

CONTENT, FUNCTION, AND STRUCTURE

Intelligence is viewed by Piaget as having three components: content, function, and structure. *Content* refers to observable behaviors—sensori-motor and conceptual—that reflect intellectual activity. The content of intelligence, because of its nature, varies considerably from age to age and from child to child. *Function* refers to those characteristics of intellectual activity—assimilation and accommodation—that are stable and continual throughout cognitive development. *Structure* refers to the inferred organizational properties (schemata) that explain the occurrence of particular behaviors. If a child is asked to compare a row of 9 checkers to a longer row of 8 checkers and determine which has more checkers, and the child says the row of 8 checkers has more, even though he counts each row, one can infer that the child does not have a complete concept of number. This would suggest that his schema for number is not yet fully developed. When confronted with a problem that pits perception against *reason*, his choice is based on perception. Eventually *reason* will prevail, but only after the determining structures have changed. These changes in *structures* are intellectual development. Flavell (1963) writes:

> Interposed between function and content, Piaget postulates the existence of cognitive structures. Structure, like content and unlike function, does indeed change with age, and these developmental changes constitute the major object of study for Piaget. What are the structures in Piaget's system? They are the organizational properties of intelligence (schèmata), organizations created through function and inferrable from the behavioral content whose nature they determine [p. 17].

Piaget has concerned himself primarily with the structure of intelligence, though he does deal with function and content to a lesser degree. His work involves the careful de-

Structure and content change—function does not

scription and analysis of *qualitative* changes in development of these cognitive structures (schemata). Presumably, qualitative structural changes in cognitive functioning most clearly are changes in intellectual functioning—what is commonly called intelligence.[1]

---

[1] It should be noted that most "intelligence" tests to a large extent sample cognitive content, not cognitive structure. By and large, they are quantitative measures, not qualitative. Piaget's conceptualizations suggest that "intelligence" tests should measure cognitive structures, as well as content, if development is to be accurately assessed.

ACTION AND COGNITIVE DEVELOPMENT

Piaget's system requires that the child *act* in the environment if cognitive development is to proceed. The development of cognitive structures is ensured only if the child assimilates and accommodates stimuli in the environment. This can only come about if the child's senses are brought to bear on the environment. When the child is acting in the environment, moving in space, manipulating objects, searching with his eyes and ears, he is taking in the raw ingredients to be assimilated and accommodated. These actions result in the development of schemata. An infant cannot learn to differentiate between a nipple and an edge of his blanket unless he *acts* on them both.

As the child becomes older, actions resulting in cognitive change become less overt. For the infant, the instrumental act may be movement of the arm and grasping. For the 9-year-old the instrumental act may be an internal one, as in adding a column of numbers. In both cases the *activity* of the child is essential for development.

Actions necessary for cognitive development to occur are clearly more than just physical movement. Actions are behaviors that stimulate the child's intellectual apparatus and may or may not be observable. These behaviors produce disequilibrium and allow assimilation and accommodation to occur.

Actions in the environment are a necessary but not sufficient condition for cognitive development. That is, the experience alone does not ensure development, but development cannot take place without it. Also necessary for development are the functional invariants, assimilation and accommodation, whose functional relationship is thought to be in part an innate or inherited (biologically linked) characteristic. Thus there are several interacting determinants of cognitive development, one of which is action.

Basically, children develop three kinds of knowledge: physical knowledge, logical-mathematical knowledge, and social-arbitrary knowledge. Each requires the child's actions, but for different reasons.

Physical Knowledge

A child acquires physical knowledge about an object while manipulating the object with his senses. For example, a child who is playing with sand may pour the sand from one container to another, feel it with his hands, or put it into his mouth. Through actions like these, children *discover* the nature of sand. Active experiences are assimilated into schemata.

In the acquisition of physical knowledge, the objects themselves (e.g., sand) "tell" the child what they can and cannot do. A child cannot construct an accurate schemata of sand unless he acts on sand. Knowledge of objects cannot be acquired from reading, looking at pictures, or listening to what people say—these are all forms of symbolic representation—but only through actions on objects. Objects permit us to construct their properties only to the extent that we *act* on them (Wadsworth, 1978).

Logical-Mathematical Knowledge

Like physical knowledge, logical-mathematical knowledge can develop only if the child acts on objects. But the respective roles of actions and objects in the construction of logical-mathematical knowledge are different. The child invents logical-mathematical knowledge; it is not inherent in objects, as physical knowledge is, but is constructed from the actions of the child on objects. The objects serve merely as a means of permitting the construction to occur.

Number concepts are examples of logical-mathematical concepts. We have all observed instances when children have been playing with sets of objects. A child may be playing with a set of 11 pennies. She puts them in a row and counts them. There are 11 of them. She puts them in a circle and counts them again. There are still 11 of them. The child stacks the pennies and counts them again. She counts 11 pennies. The child puts the pennies in a box and shakes them up. Removed from the box and counted, again, there are 11 pennies. Through many active experiences like this, children eventually construct the concept that the number of objects in a set remains the same regardless of the arrangement of the individual elements. This is an invention of logical-mathematical knowledge.

In the development of logical-mathematical knowledge, the nature of the objects is not critical, only that there are groups of objects for the child to manipulate. The concept the child was developing in the preceding example could have developed as easily using stones, crayons, pots and pans, or flowers. As such experiences are repeated over and over, in different settings and with different materials, these concepts become more refined. Like physical knowledge, logical-mathematical knowledge is not acquired from reading or listening to people talk. It is acquired from actions on objects.

Social-Arbitrary Knowledge

Social-arbitrary knowledge is knowledge developed by humankind. It includes knowledge of rules, laws, morals, values, ethics, and language systems. This knowledge evolves within cultures. It cannot be extracted from actions on objects in the manner of physical and logical-mathematical knowledge. Social-arbitrary knowledge is constructed by children from their actions on (interactions with) other people. As children interact with each other and with adults, opportunities for the construction of social-arbitrary knowledge are encountered.[2]

According to Piagetian theory, all knowledge is physical knowledge, logical-mathematical knowledge, or social-arbitrary knowledge (Wadsworth, 1978). Of central importance in the construction of knowledge are the child's *actions* on objects and interactions with people. Knowledge cannot be derived directly from reading or from listening to people talk (e.g., teachers). Knowledge can be acquired only from *experience* with relevant objects, and cannot be acquired from representations of objects and events (e.g., by written or spoken words). These are major implications for educational practice.

The child is more dependent on physical and sensorial experience in the earlier years of life when he does not possess the power of symbolic representation (language). At this time, interaction with the environment is completely on a sensory and motor level. The child acts directly on objects in the environment. Development proceeds as the infant explores his environment via his reflexes. A variety of objects are placed in the mouth or sucked via the sucking reflex. Objects are grasped. These active reflexive behaviors allow the infant to make his first differentiations of the environment. These acts allow the child to develop internal sensori-motor representations (schemata) of the objects as he makes discriminations.

At a later age, the child's actions on the environment will be mediated by internalized symbols and language and will

---

[2] Chapter Nine, on the development of moral reasoning, deals in some depth with the development of moral concepts, which are one kind of social-arbitrary knowledge.

be less overt. Actions will be less sensori-motor and more conceptual. Nonetheless, the active participation of the child remains necessary for cognitive development. The child learning to add a column of figures is acting on the environment. The behavior is covert, but nonetheless an action.

MOTIVATION

Piaget has dealt extensively with the question of motivation of cognitive behavior: what energizes behavior and provides the direction for behavior. He rejects the notion of extrinsic "needs" (external forces) as being responsible for motivating cognitive behavior in the organism. In doing this, he rejects the concept of reinforcement that is central to behaviorism and learning theory. The "need" to engage in cognitive activity is, according to Piaget, an intrinsic need—motivation is from within the organism, not from without. This comes about, Piaget says, because cognitive structures, once developed and functioning, perpetuate themselves by more functioning. In the acts of assimilation and accommodation, there is an intrinsic tendency to assimilate and accommodate the environment. Piaget writes (*The Origins of Intelligence in Children*, 1952, pp. 45-46):

> ... in the young child the principal needs are of a functional category. The functioning of the organs engenders, through its very existence ... a series of vicarious needs whose complexity transcends, from the very beginning, simple organic satisfaction (primary needs) ... the principal motive power of intellectual activity thus becoming the need to incorporate things into the subject's schemata ... the basic fact is not need of such but rather the act of assimilation.

When children encounter experiences that are not consistent with what they expect or predict, the stage is set for disequilibration, the upsetting of their intellectual stability (equilibrium). If disequilibrium *within the child* occurs, the mechanisms of assimilation and accommodation are activated. The child "seeks out" the environment in an effort to make sense of, or assimilate, the disequilibrating experience. The keys to motivation of cognitive development are disequilibration and assimilation. According to Piaget, motivation is intrinsic.

PERIODS OF DEVELOPMENT

In the broadest sense, Piaget asserts throughout his work that cognitive and intellectual changes are the result of a developmental process. Piaget's general "hypothesis" is simply that cognitive development is a coherent process of successive qualitative changes of cognitive structures (schemata), each structure and its concommitant change deriving logically and inevitably from the preceding one. New schemata do not replace prior ones; they incorporate them, resulting in a qualitative change. If the young boy who classified a cow as a dog suddenly at some later time decides that the cow is no longer a dog, but a new object called a "cow," he does not *replace* schemata. What he may do is create a new schema (accommodate) for cowlike objects, while retaining his old, but now modified, schema for dogs. Thus a change has occurred that results in a qualitatively superior set of schemata, the current schemata incorporating the previous ones.

For purposes of conceptualizing cognitive growth, intellectual development can be divided into four broad periods (and other subperiods, stages, and substages).[3] Piaget has

---

[3] The number of stages one divides development into is somewhat arbitrary. Piaget has on different occasions divided development into three, four, or six major stages, each time with a number of substages. The author has, for his purposes, divided development into four stages.

been criticized for the use of periods or stages in his theory. Those who object to his use of stages *probably* do so out of misunderstanding. Piaget does not suggest that children move from discrete stage to discrete stage in development, as one moves from one step to another while walking upstairs. Cognitive development flows along, but the defining stage is useful to the observer in conceptualizing the developmental process. The researcher and theorist can divide the long period of development into periods of shorter length, and in that way development can be analyzed and, in some ways, conceptualized more efficiently. This does not in any way deny the continuity of development over its entire course, nor does it mean that the periods are selected without a rationale.

Piaget (*The Psychology of Intelligence,* 1963) broadly summarizes the periods (or stages) of cognitive development as:

1. *The period of sensori-motor intelligence (0-2 years).* During this period behavior is primarily motor. The child does not yet "think" conceptually, though "cognitive" development is seen.

2. *The period of preoperational thought (2-7 years).* This period is characterized by the development of language and rapid conceptual development.

3. *The period of concrete operations (7-11 years).* During these years the child develops the ability to apply logical thought to *concrete* problems.

4. *The period of formal operations (11-15 years or older).* During this period the child's cognitive *structures* reach their greatest level of development, and the child becomes able to apply logic to all classes of problems.

Development is thought to flow along in a cumulative manner, each new step in development becoming integrated with previous steps. The behaviors described are

only typical behaviors of a given age, period, or stage.
Piaget writes (*The Origins of Intelligence in Children*,
1952, p. 329):

> In a general way, the fact should be emphasized that the
> behavior patterns characteristic of the different stages do not
> succeed each other in a linear way (those of a given stage
> disappearing at the time when those of the following one take
> form) but in the manner of the layers of a pyramid (upright, or
> upside down), the new behavior patterns simply being added
> to the old ones to complete, correct, or combine with them.

It should be mentioned again that the stages are not independent of each other in actual development. Also, the
chronological ages during which children can be expected
to develop behavior representative of a particular stage are
not fixed. The age spans that have been suggested by
Piaget are *normative* and denote the times during which
most children can be expected to display the intellectual
behaviors that are characteristic of the particular stage.
The typical child enters the preoperational period around
the age of 2. Although some enter the period earlier—a
very small percentage of 1-year-olds enter the preoperational period—other children do not enter the preoperational period until age 3 or 4. With severely "retarded"
children, development may be even slower. The behaviors
that will be described for each stage are *only* typical for
the age groups. The norms that have been established by
Piaget are for samples of children in Geneva, and do not
necessarily hold for American samples. Piaget assumes that
the fixed order of appearance (of structures of behavior)
implies nothing concerning the experiential or hereditary
basis for the order. The age at which the stages occur can
vary with the nature of both the individual's experience
and his hereditary potential (Ibid., p. 255). Progress
through stages is not automatic (as in maturation theory).

One aspect of the stage theory of Piaget is "fixed." According to Piaget, every child *must* pass through the stages of cognitive development in the same order. A child cannot move intellectually from the preoperational stage to the period of formal operations without passing through the period of concrete operations.

While this is true, the rates at which children pass through the stages may not be identical, due to experiential or hereditary factors. "Bright" children may go through the stages rapidly; "dull" children more slowly, some never reaching or completing the last stages (formal operations).

While a concept of stages of intellectual development is used, it should be remembered that the range of intellectual behaviors within a particular stage is quite large. That is, while the child develops the use of language during the preoperational period (2 to 7 years), it is expected that language usage at age 7 will be qualitatively different than at age 2.

In the early part of the preoperational stage, language ability is being formed and organized. Thus, the language behaviors of the 3-year-old typically lack the organization and stability of the 7-year-old, though they will both demonstrate characteristics of the stage. Thus it is that behaviors early in a stage, or early in the development of a particular intellectual function, can be expected to have less stability and to be less sophisticated than in later periods.

PERIOD TRANSITION FACTORS

So far it has been made clear that, according to Piaget, cognitive development follows a "fixed" course wherein the child moves progressively through four major stages.

From birth through adulthood the structures of intelligence, schemata, are constantly developing as the child
spontaneously acts on the environment and assimilates and
accommodates to an increasing array of stimuli in his environment. Are there other factors that act to influence
the course of cognitive development? According to Piaget,
there are.

Piaget (1961) suggests there are four broad factors that
are related to all cognitive development: (1) maturation,
(2) physical experience, (3) social interaction, and (4) a
general progression of equilibrium (Ibid., p. 277). Piaget
views each of these factors and their interaction as necessary conditions for cognitive development, but none of
them, by themselves, is seen as sufficient to ensure cognitive development. Movement within and between stages of
development is a function of these factors and their actions.

Maturation

For Piaget, maturation is a factor in cognitive development. The main contribution of maturation to cognitive
development is in neurological growth (the growth of brain
and nervous system tissue) and the development of the en-
docrine system (Piaget, 1969). While maturation clearly
plays a part in development, its importance is somewhat
minimized by Piaget:

> The maturation of the nervous system can do no more than
> determine the totality of possibilities and impossibilities at a
> given stage. A particular social environment remains indispens-
> able for the realization of these possibilities. It follows that
> their realization can be accelerated or retarded as a function of
> cultural or educational conditions [Inhelder and Piaget, 1958,
> p. 337].

Thus, maturation factors (or inherited factors) place

broad constraints on cognitive development. These constraints change as maturation proceeds. Realization of the "potential" implied by these constraints at any point in development depends on the child's actions on his environment.

Physical Experience

A second factor in cognitive development is physical experience, the child's actions on objects. The child must have experience with objects and stimuli in the environment on which he can spontaneously act. Assimilation and accommodation cannot take place unless there is interaction between the organism and the environment. Not only must the child have experience, but he must act on the environment, not just react to it (as in S-R learning theory). The growth of cognitive structures (schemata) via assimilation and accommodation requires that the child interact with the environment. Early in life, interaction with the environment is primarily on a sensori-motor level. The child manipulates the environment in a direct manner. The hand grasps objects, the mouth sucks objects, the eyes explore. As the child develops and is capable of reasoning, thought becomes one form of "action" on objects. Thinking and reasoning are forms of internal representation. During the later periods of development they begin to play a major role in the child's construction of knowledge. To the extent that the child actively assimilates and accommodates to the environment, he will develop cognitively. Schemata cannot develop unless they are aroused by disequilibrium to activate assimilation and accommodation. This requires the *child's* action.

Social Interaction

Another factor in cognitive development is social interaction. By social interaction, Piaget means the interchange of ideas between people. This is particularly important in the development of social-arbitrary knowledge. The concepts or schemata that people develop can be classified as two types: those that have sensorially available physical referents (they can be seen, heard, and so on), and those that do not have such referents. The concept "tree" has physical referents; the concept "honesty" does not. A child can develop a socially acceptable concept of "tree" (physical knowledge) relatively independent of others, for referents are usually available. But the same child cannot develop a acceptable concept of "honesty" (social-arbitrary knowledge) independent of others. To the extent that concepts are "arbitrary" or socially defined, the child is dependent on social interaction for the construction and validation of his concepts.

Social interaction can be of many types. There is interaction with peers, parents, and other adults. The events that take place in a schoolroom are most frequently the interaction of students with other students and their teachers. There is also the interaction with parents and others in the environment. All of these are important in cognitive development.

Equilibration

The previous concepts of maturation, experience, and social interaction do not suffice to explain cognitive development. Mental behaviors are observed that suggest the child contributes an organizational, or regulating, quality to development. Piaget (1961) writes:

> . . . if the development depends . . . on internal factors (maturation) . . . and . . . on external factors (physical or social), it is self-evident that these internal and external factors equilibrate each other . . . We believe . . . that the mental equi-

librium and even the biological one presumes an activity of the subject . . . It consists in a sort of matching, oriented towards compensation . . . [p. 279] .

Piaget and Inhelder (1969) also say:

An internal mechanism (though it cannot be reduced to heredity alone and has no preestablished plan, since there is in fact construction) is observable at the time of each partial construction and each transition from one stage to the next. It is a process of equilibrium . . . of self-regulation; that is, a series of active compensations on the part of the subject in response to external disturbances and an adjustment that is both retroactive (loop systems or feedback) and anticipation, constituting a permanent system of compensations [p. 157].

Thus, equilibration (attaining equilibrium) is seen as an internal self-regulating system that operates to reconcile the roles of maturation, experience, and social interaction.

While maturation, experience, social interaction, and equilibration are all necessary for cognitive development to proceed, none by itself is sufficient for development to occur. They must all be present and *interact*. Maturational potential without active experience will not result in development. Active experience without maturation will not result in development. There must be an interaction or mix of the ingredients. For this reason, Piaget is most accurately classified as an "interactionist" rather than as an environmentalist or maturationist.

SUMMARY

Heredity, according to Piaget, most influences cognitive development in that it places broad constraints on development. Development proceeds as a function of the interaction of endowment and experience. The child must act on the environment.

Intelligence is seen as having three components: content, function, and structure. Piaget has primarily studied the development of schemata, the structures of intelligence.

Motivation, according to Piaget, is an "intrinsic" force that is self-activating once assimilation and accommodation begin. Development proceeds through four major stages. It is both fixed and continuous. All persons develop through the same stages in the same way, though not necessarily at the same rates. Four factors were described as being "necessary" for mental development: maturation, experience, social interaction, and equilibration.

Chapter Three

The Sensori-Motor Period

Mental development is a process that begins the day the infant is born (and possibly sooner). This does not mean that the child is born thinking (internally representing objects in the mind), but it does mean that the sensori-motor behaviors that occur from birth on are necessary for and instrumental in later cognitive development. To look at it another way, intellectual behavior at any age evolves directly from prior levels of behavior. Thus the roots of all intellectual development are in early sensori-motor behavior.

Piaget has carefully described development during the first two years of life in several books. From his observations and writings, it is clear that the structures of intelligence begin to evolve during infancy. At birth, the child can perform only simple reflex behaviors. Two years later he is typically beginning to talk (symbolic representation), and he has clearly evolved intellectual operations. The child can solve most sensori-motor problems, i.e., he can get objects he wants; he can use one object to retrieve another; he can mentally "invent" means (behaviors) that will permit him to do things he wants (attain ends).

The 2-year-old is cognitively different from the infant at

birth. The infant is born with a few sensori-motor schemata (sucking, grasping, crying). The same child, two years
later, bears little resemblance intellectually to the infant.
At 2 he has a comparatively much larger and more sophisticated array of schemata. The evolution that occurs is
primarily a function of the child's sensori-motor actions on
the environment, resulting in ongoing assimilation and accommodation, that in turn results in qualitative and quantitative changes in schemata. Piaget (1968) writes:

> The period that extends from birth to the acquisition of
> language is marked by an extraordinary development of the
> mind. Its importance is sometimes underestimated because it
> is not accompanied by words that permit a step-by-step pur-
> suit of the progress of intelligence and the emotions, as is the
> case later on. This early mental development nonetheless de-
> termines the entire course of psychological evolution... At the
> starting point of this development the neonate grasps every-
> thing to himself—or, in more precise terms, to his own body—
> whereas at the termination of the period, i.e., when language
> and thought begin, he is for all practical purposes but one
> element or entity among others in a universe that he has grad-
> ually constructed himself, and which hereafter he will experi-
> ence as external to himself [pp. 8-9].

To understand that the development of language in the
2-year-old is related to earlier sensori-motor development,
the observer must carefully observe behavior during the
first two years of life. The evolution that occurs is a re-
markably smooth succession of stages, each stage incorporating the previous stage, each marking a new advance.

Piaget (1952, 1954, 1967) divides the sensori-motor period into six stages (see Table 1) in which progressively
more complex patterns of intellectual behavior evolve.

The remainder of this chapter will present aspects of the

six stages of sensori-motor development. The general characteristics of each stage will be discussed. These will include the progressive development of the child's *object* concept and his concept of *causality*, two of the most important indicators of intellectual development during this period.

What has previously been said about periods of development applies equally well to the stages of development about to be discussed. As behaviors evolve that are representative of a more advanced stage, the behaviors of previous stages are not totally displaced. Old, less sophisticated behaviors will still occur. Regarding new stages, Piaget (1964) writes:

> The new stage would thus be defined by the fact that the child becomes capable of certain behavior patterns of which he was up to then incapable; it is not the fact that he renounces the behavior patterns of the preceding stages, even if they are contrary to the new ones or contradictory to them from the observer's point of view [p. 299].

STAGE 1 (0-1 MONTH)

Beginning at birth and throughout most of the first stage of sensori-motor development, the behavior of the typical infant is entirely reflexive. The basic reflexes that the infant is born with are sucking, grasping, crying, and movement of arms, trunk, and head. When the infant is stimulated, his reflexes respond. Thus, when an object is put in the infant's mouth, he sucks on it, regardless of what it is. When an object contacts the palm of the infant's hand, he grasps it, regardless of what it is. There is no evidence that the infant, behaving so, can differentiate between objects. His reflex responses are more or less the same to all objects. A blanket is sucked on as vigorously as a milk-pro-

TABLE 1

Characteristics of Development During the Sensori-Motor Period

Stage	General	Object Concept	Space	Causality
1 Reflex 0-1 mo.	Reflex activity	No differentiation of self from other objects	Egocentric	Egocentric
2 First differentiations 1-4 mos.	Hand-mouth coordination; differentiation via sucking, grasping	No special behavior re vanished objects; no differentiation of movement of self and external objects	Changes in perspective seen as changes in objects	No differentiation of movement of self and external objects
3 Reproduction, 4-8 mos.	Eye-hand coordination; reproduction of interesting events	Anticipates positions of moving objects	Space externalized; no spacial relationships of objects	Self seen as cause of all events

4 Coordination of schemata, 8-12 mos.	Coordination of schemata; application of known means to new problems; anticipation	Object permanence; searches for vanished objects; reverses bottle to get nipple	Perceptual constancy of size and shape of objects	Elementary externalization of causality
5 Experimentation, 12-18 mos.	Discovery of new means through experimentation	Considers sequential displacements while searching for vanished objects	Aware of relationships between objects in space, between objects and self	Self seen as object among objects and self as object of actions
6 Representation, 18-24 mos.	Representation; invention of new means via internal combinations	Images of absent objects, representation of displacements	Aware of movements not perceived; representation of spatial relationships	Representative causality; causes and effects inferred

ducing nipple. The hand grasps what comes into it, be it someone's finger or a toy. No distinction is made between stimuli. Thus, during this stage, the infant *assimilates* all stimuli through the reflex systems. At birth, all stimulus events are incorporated (assimilated) into primitive reflexive *schemata* in an undifferentiated manner.

Within a few weeks of birth, simple *accommodations* on the part of the child are usually observable. At birth the infant sucks on what is placed in its mouth. A nipple is sucked on when presented. Soon the infant begins to "search" for the nipple if it cannot be found; in effect, accommodating to the environment. The "searching" by the infant is a behavior that was not present at birth and cannot be attributed to any reflex system. There is no "searching" reflex; there is only a sucking reflex. Thus the active searching can be viewed as a change in reflex behavior on the part of the infant—an *accommodation.*

The innate, random reflex acts observable during the first stage undergo modification as a result of their repetitive use and interaction with the environment. While the young infant seems to be only exercising his reflexes when behaving, and no intellectual behaviors are observable, the *use* of the reflexes is essential for development during the stage and for the development of cognitive structures that are to follow. From the beginning, acts of assimilation and accommodation are present.

Object Concept

One of Piaget's important beliefs is that all concepts including the object concept are not innate. That is, the awareness that objects are more or less permanent, and are not destroyed when they disappear, is not an inherited characteristic. He believes this awareness of objects is developed out of sensori-motor experiences little by little

(Piaget, 1954, p. 4). In effect the child must reconstruct the universe of objects through his experiences. At birth, the infant has no awareness of objects other than on a reflexive level. Indeed, the infant is unable to differentiate between himself and the environment. The infant has no concept of objects. Any object presented by the external environment is merely something to suck, to grasp, or to look at—something that evokes an undifferentiated reflexive response.

Concept of Causality

Causality, an awareness of cause and effect relationships, is another important concept that develops during the sensori-motor period. At birth the child is totally egocentric[1] and not aware of causality at all. It is not until later that awareness of causality begins to evolve.

STAGE 2 (1-4 MONTHS)

The second stage of sensori-motor development begins when the reflexive behaviors of the previous stage begin to be modified. During this stage several new behaviors appear. Thumb-sucking becomes habitual and reflects the development of some hand-mouth coordination; moving objects are followed with the eyes (eye coordination); and the head is moved in the direction of sounds (eye-ear coordination).

---

[1] Egocentrism is one of Piaget's most important concepts. In general it refers to the cognitive state in which the individual sees the world only from his point of view, without being aware that other points of view exist. Thus it is a state that the egocentric cannot be aware of. For the infant, egocentrism means there is an absence of self-perception, of the self being an object in a world of objects. This is only overcome when the infant's concept of object develops and subsequently permits the development of self-perception.

Early in Stage 1, the infant's responses to stimuli are purely reflexive. No differentiation is initially made between stimuli. Toward the end of Stage 1 the infant begins to distinguish between objects, a behavior not present at birth. For example, the infant actively sucks on a milk-producing nipple (when hungry), but rejects other objects that are placed in its mouth if it wants milk. A reflex has been modified, indicating that the infant has made an *accommodation* to the environment. Where a primitive sucking *schema* that did not permit differentiation had existed, a more sophisticated schema permitting differentiation now exists. Changes in behavior of this type are the first observable, if primitive, signs of the internal organization of and adaptation to the environment.

Habitual thumb-sucking is a behavior typically acquired during this stage (Piaget, *The Origins of Intelligence in Children*, 1952, p. 48). This new behavior requires hand-mouth coordination, an ability that the infant does not have during the first month. Prior to this time, thumb-sucking that occurs is usually a random or chance occurrence; the thumb happens to get into the mouth. Habituation of the activity cannot be explained by reflexes alone. It can only be explained by the child's discovery of sensori-motor relationships while acting on the environment.

Piaget (*The Origins of Intelligence in Children*, 1952, p. 53) illustrates the transition from random to clearly coordinated thumb-sucking:

Observation 19.—At 0;1 (4)[2] after the 6 P.M. meal Laurent is wide awake (as was not the case at the preceding meals) and not completely satisfied. First he makes vigorous sucking-like

[2] 0;1 (4): Designations of this type make reference to the age of the child at the time of the observation, with years, months, days being referred to in that order. Laurent was 1 month, 4 days old at the time of observation.

movements, then his right hand may be seen approaching his mouth, touching his lower lip and finally being grasped. But as only the index finger was grasped, the hand fell out again. Shortly afterward it returned. This time the thumb was in the mouth while the index finger was placed between the gums and the upper lip. The hand then moves 5 cm. away from the mouth only to reenter it; now the thumb is grasped and the other fingers remain outside. Laurent then is motionless and sucks vigorously, drooling so much that after a few moments he is removed. A fourth time the hand approaches and three fingers enter the mouth. The hand leaves again and reenters a fifth time. As the thumb has again been grasped, sucking is resumed. I then remove the hand and place it near his waist. Laurent seems to give up sucking and gazes ahead, contented and satisfied. But after a few minutes the lips move and the hand approaches them again. This time there is a series of setbacks; the fingers are placed on the chin and lower lip. The index finger enters the mouth twice (consequently the sixth and seventh time this has succeeded). The eighth time the hand enters the mouth, the thumb alone is retained and sucking continues. I again remove the hand. Again lip movements cease, new attempts ensue, success results for the ninth and tenth time, after which the experiment is interrupted.

Laurent's thumb-sucking is rapidly becoming habitual. The behavior, since it is directed by the child, is different from all reflex behavior at birth. Such coordination implies an *accommodation* on the part of the child.

On the matter of thumb-sucking, Piaget (Ibid., p. 48) writes:

> When the child systematically sucks his thumb, no longer due to chance contacts but through coordination between hand and mouth, this may be called acquired accommodation. Neither the reflexes of the mouth nor of the hand can be provided such coordination by heredity (there is no instinct to suck the thumb!) and experience alone explains its formation.

During the second stage coordinations develop in the use of his eyes. The child begins to follow moving objects with the eyes. Piaget provides an example (Ibid., p. 63):

Observation 28.—Jacqueline at 0;0(16) does not follow with her eyes the flame of a match 20 cm. away. Only her expression changes at the sight of it and then she moves her head as though to find the light again. She does not succeed despite the dim light in the room. At 0;0(24), on the other hand, she follows the match perfectly under the same conditions. The subsequent days her eyes follow the movements of my hand, a moving handkerchief, etc. From this date she can remain awake without crying, gazing ahead.

The ability to visually follow moving objects is not present at birth. As can be seen in Jacqueline's case, this ability is acquired.

Coordination between hearing and vision also develops at this time. Discriminations between sounds begin to occur. This is evident when children begin to move their heads in the direction of sounds, and when faces of people are clearly associated with sounds of the same person.

Observation 48.—From 0;1(26) on the other hand, Laurent turns in the right direction as soon as he hears my voice (even if he has not seen me just before) and seems satisfied when he has discovered my face even when it is immobile. At 0;1(27) he looks successively at his father, his mother, and again at his father after hearing my voice. It therefore seems that he ascribes this voice to a visually familiar face. At 0;2(14) he observes Jacqueline at 1.90 to 2 meters, at the sound of her voice; same observation at 0;2(21). At 0;3(1) I squat before him while he is in his mother's arms and I make the sound bzz (which he likes). He looks to his left, then to his right, then ahead, then below him; then he catches sight of my hair and lowers his eyes until he sees my motionless face. Finally he smiles. This last observation may be considered as definitely indicating identification of the voice and visual image of the person [Ibid., pp. 82-83].

These examples illustrate some of the cognitive differences between a typical child during the first month of life (Stage 1) and the next few months (Stage 2). The younger child makes undifferentiated reflex responses to stimuli. The older child makes primitive sensori-motor differentiations and acquires limited sensori-motor coordinations. These developments come about as the infant acts using his reflexes. Assimilation and accommodation produce initial changes in schemata.

Object Concept

During the second period of sensori-motor development the child evokes an awareness of objects that was not present during the first period. As was said earlier, the child tries to look at the objects he hears, indicating a coordination between vision and hearing. In addition, the child may continue to follow the path of an object with his eyes after it has disappeared from view. The following example from Piaget (1954) illustrates acquired visual following:

> Thus, Lucienne, at 0;3(9) sees me at the extreme left of her visual field and smiles vaguely. She then looks in different directions, in front of her and to the right, but constantly returns to the place in which she sees me and dwells on it every time for a moment [p. 10].

> At 0;4(26) she takes the breast but turns when I call her and smiles at me. Then she resumes nursing but several times in succession, despite my silence, she turns directly to the position from which she can see me. She does it again after a pause of a few minutes. Then I withdraw; when she turns without finding me her expression is one of mingled disappointment and expectation [pp. 10-11].

Lucienne (one of Piaget's daughters) demonstrates clearly that she has coordination between hearing and vision. She locates visually the source of sounds. In addition, she is able to return and visually locate objects that have left her field of vision.

Intentionality

A number of new sensori-motor coordinations develop in Stage 2. The range of responses the infant makes increases. While advances have been made, the child's behavior still lacks *intention* in the sense that he initiates behaviors directed at certain ends. Behaviors are still primarily reflexive (though modified) and goals are set off only *after* behavior sequences are begun. Piaget writes (*The Origins of Intelligence in Children*, 1952, p.143):

> As long as action is entirely determined by directly perceived sensorial images, there can be no question of intention. Even when the child grasps an object in order to look at it, one cannot infer that there is a conscious purpose. It is with the appearance of. . . deferred reactions that the purpose of the action, ceasing to be in some way directly perceived, presupposes a continuity in searching, and consequently a beginning of intention.

Intentionality of behavior can only be inferred when the initiation of behaviors is not a reflex act or a simple repetition of preceding behavior.

Thus, the initial steps in intellectual development have begun. The child's actions in the environment, resulting in assimilations and accommodation, have produced primitive structural changes permitting simple sensori-motor coordinations. In the next stage these advances will be elaborated and surpassed through the same processes.

STAGE 3 (4-8 MONTHS)

During Stage 3, the child's behaviors become increasingly oriented toward objects and events beyond his body. The child grasps and manipulates all objects he can reach, signifying coordination between vision and tactile senses. Prior to this time, the infant's behavior has been oriented primarily toward himself. He has been unable to effectively distinguish himself from other objects on a sensori-motor level. He has been unable to coordinate the movement of his hands with his eyes.

Another characteristic of the third stage is that infants reproduce events that occur that are unusual to them. When interesting experiences occur, they try to repeat them. A cord attached to overhead bells is pulled repeatedly. Grasping and striking acts are repeated intentionally. There are clear attempts to sustain and repeat acts. Piaget (Ibid.) refers to this phenomenon as *reproductive assimilation*: the infant tries to reproduce events that are of interest to him. As an illustration, Piaget (Ibid.) writes:

Observation 104.—At 0;3(29)Laurent grasps a paper knife which he sees for the first time; he looks at it a moment and then swings it while holding it in his right hand. During these movements the object happens to rub against the wicker of the bassinet: Laurent then waves his arms vigorously and obviously tries to reproduce the sound he has heard, but without understanding the necessity of contact between the paper knife and the wicker and, consequently, without achieving this contact otherwise than by chance.

At 0;4(3) same reactions, but Laurent looks at the object at the time when it happens to rub against the wicker of the bassinet. The same still occurs at 0;4(5) but there is slight progress towards systematization.

Finally, at 0;4(6) the movement becomes intentional; as soon as the child has the object in his hand he rubs it with regularity against the wicker of the bassinet. . .[pp. 168-169].

When a child successfully repeats previous behaviors, as Laurent did in the example, primitive sensori-motor intentionality is evident.

Intentionality

One of the characteristics of the sensori-motor period is the child's progress from non-intentional behavior to a type of intentional behavior. During the second period of sensori-motor development, intentional behavior is not evident. At that time behavior is random and elicited by stimulation. It is not designed to attain a goal or object. During Stage 3, the child begins to engage in a type of goal-directed (intentional) behavior. He tries to repeat unusual and interesting events. In Stage 3, goals are established only *after* behaviors have begun. The infant's goals become established only during the repetitions of behaviors, and consequently, the intentionality (goal direction) is after the fact, so to speak, after behavior has begun. In later stages (Stage 4), the infant *initiates* a behavior sequence with a goal to be attained already in mind, and selects means that he thinks will attain the goal. Intentionality is present at the beginning of the sequence, and thus the behavior is not a mere repetition of a previous behavior, but an intentional act. Thus while behavior in Stage 3 is for the first time intentional, it is not intentional until after behavior sequences have begun.

Object Concept

During period 3 the child begins to anticipate positions objects will pass through while they are moving. This indicates that the child's awareness of the permanence of objects is developing. The following example from Piaget (1954) illustrates this:

> Observation 6.—Laurent's reaction to falling objects still seems to be nonexistent at 0;5(24): he does not follow with his eyes any of the objects which I drop in front of him . . .
>
> At 0;5(30) no reaction to the fall of a box of matches. The same is true at 0;6(0), but when he drops the box himself he searches for it next to him with his eyes (he is lying down) . . .
>
> At 0;6(7) he holds an empty match box in his hand. When it falls his eyes search for it even if they have not followed the beginning of the fall; he turns his head in order to see it on the sheet. Same reaction at 0;6(9) with a rattle . . .
>
> At 0;7(29) he searches on the floor for everything I drop above him, if he has in the least perceived the beginning of the movement of falling . . . [pp. 14-15] .

In the example, Laurent by 8 months of age is looking for objects in places where he predicts they have fallen. He is anticipating positions falling objects will assume, demonstrating a more sophisticated schema of object than in previous stages.

Concept of Causality

During Stage 3 the child remains egocentric. He sees himself as the primary cause of all activity. The following example illustrates the child's egocentric awareness of causality during Stage 3. Piaget (1954) writes:

> At 0;7(8) Laurent is seated and I place a large cushion within his reach. I scratch the cushion. He laughs. Afterward I move my hand five cm. from the cushion, between it and his own hands, in such a way that if he pushed it slightly it would press against the cushion. As soon as I pause, Laurent strikes the cushion, arches, swings his head, etc. True, subsequently he

does sometimes grasp my hand. But it is only in order to strike it, shake it, etc., and he does not once try to move it forward or put it in contact with the cushion.

At a certain moment he scratches my hand; on the other hand, he does not scratch the cushion although this behavior is familiar to him [p. 245].

Clearly, Laurent believes he alone can cause events. He is not aware that his father's hand is causing the interesting sound when it is in contact with the cushion. He shakes his father's hand to make the sound; he scratches the hand. He acts on the hand and on the cushion, but never on the two together. To the child at this stage, he himself is the cause of all events.

STAGE 4 (8-12 MONTHS)

Toward the end of the first year of life, behavior patterns emerge that constitute the first clear acts of intelligence. The infant begins to use means to attain ends; he begins to anticipate events, demonstrating prevision. Objects take on a noticeable measure of permanence for the child. He begins to search for objects that he sees disappear. Also, he comes to see that other objects in the environment can be sources of activity (causality).

Prior to this stage, behavior has always been a direct action of the child on objects. Interesting acts are prolonged or repeated. That is, a single *schema* had been used to evoke a behavioral response. During Stage 4 the child begins to coordinate two familiar schemata in generating a single act: he begins to use means to attain ends that are not immediately attainable in a direct way. Children can be seen to set aside one object (means) to get to another object (end). A pillow is moved out of the way to reach a toy. There is an *intentional* selection of means prior to the initiation of behavior. The end is established from the beginning, the means being used precisely in order to reach the end. The following example from Piaget (*The Origins of Intelligence in Children*, 1952) illustrates the means-ends coordination that develops:

> Observation 121.—At 0;8(20) Jacqueline tries to grasp a ciga-rette case which I present to her. I then slide it between the crossed strings which attach her dolls to the hood (of her bassinet). She tries to reach it directly. Not succeeding, she immediately looks for the strings which are not in her hands and of which she only saw the part in which the cigarette case is entangled. She looks in front of her, grasps the strings, pulls and shakes them, etc. The cigarette case then falls and she grasps it.
>
> Second experiment: same reaction, but without first trying to grasp the object directly [p. 215].

In the example Jacqueline pulls the strings (means) to attain the cigarette case (end). Clearly this is an intentional act from the outset. Means and ends (two schemata) are coordinated in one action.

During Stage 4, the infant shows clear signs of anticipation of events. Certain "signs" are recognized as being associated with certain actions that follow the signs. These actions illustrate prevision and the "meaning" of certain events.

> Observation 132.—At 0;8(6) Laurent recognizes by a certain noise caused by air that he is nearing the end of his feeding and, instead of insisting on drinking to the last drop, he rejects his bottle . . .
>
> Observation 133.—At 0;9(15) Jacqueline wails or cries when she sees the person seated next to her get up or move away a little (giving the impression of leaving) . . .
>
> At 1;1(10) she has a slight scratch which is disinfected with alcohol. She cries, chiefly from fear. Subsequently, as soon as she again sees the bottle of alcohol she recommences to cry,

knowing what is in store for her. Two days later, same reaction, as soon as she sees the bottle and even before it is opened [Ibid., pp. 248-249].

Such behavior clearly demonstrates anticipation or prevision on the part of the child. An action is anticipated that is independent of the action in progress. During preceding stages actions of the child were *always* dependent on the immediate actions in the environment. Jacqueline would cry when alcohol was put on a cut, not before it was put on.

Object Concept

The most important acquisition of this stage is undoubtedly that of the constancies of shape and size of objects. Commenting on shape and size constancy, Piaget and Inhelder (1956) write:

> In fact, the *constancy of shapes* results from their sensorimotor construction at the time of the coordination of perspectives. During the first period (0-4 mos.) . . . when objects change their perspective such alterations are perceived (by the child) not as changes in the point of view of the subject relative to the object, but as actual transformations of the objects themselves. The baby waggling his head before a hanging object behaves as if he acted upon it by jerking about, and it is not until the age of about 8-9 months that he really explores the perspective effects of actual displacements. Now it is just about this age (8-9 mos.) that he is first able . . . to reverse a feeding bottle presented to him wrong way round. That is. to attribute a fixed shape to a permanent solid.
>
> As for *size constancy* it is linked with the coordination of perceptually controlled movements. All through the first period (0-4 mos.) the child makes no distinction between movements of the object and those of his body . . . In the course of the second period (Stage 3 and 4) the subject begins to distinguish his own movements from those of the object. Here is

found the beginning . . . of searching for objects when they disappear. It is in terms of this grouping of movements, and the permanence attributed to the object, that the latter acquires fixed dimensions and its size is estimated more or less correctly, regardless of whether it is near or distant [p. 11].

As with other concepts, those of size and constancy develop in the expected manner. Different perspectives on objects appear to the 4-month-old child to change the shape and size of the objects. Not until Stage 4 are shape and size of objects stabilized concepts for the child.

During period 4 a new dimension in the object concept of the child appears. Up until this time, if an object such as a rattle is placed under a blanket while the child is looking on, the child does not search after it. If an object is out of sight, it no longer exists to the child. Between the ages of 8 and 10 months (approximately) the child begins to search for objects that disappear, indicating the child is aware the objects exist even when they cannot be seen. The rattle hidden under the blanket is retrieved. The following illustration from Piaget (1954) illustrates this new awareness of object permanence and some of its limitations:

Observation 40.—At 0;10(18) Jacqueline is seated on a mattress without anything to disturb or distract her (no coverlets, etc.). I take her parrot from her hands and hide it twice in succession under the mattress, on her left, in A. Both times Jacqueline looks for the object immediately and grabs it. Then I take it from her hands and move it very slowly before her eyes to the corresponding place on her right, under the mattress, in B (sequential displacement). Jacqueline watches this movement very attentively, but at the moment when the parrot disappears in B, she turns to her left and looks where it was before, in A.

During the next four attempts I hide the parrot in B every time without having first placed it in A. Each time Jacqueline watches me attentively. Nevertheless each time she immediately tries to rediscover the object in A; she turns the mattress over and examines it conscientiously . . . [p. 51].

Clearly, Jacqueline searches for objects that disappear. To do this she must have a concept that objects still exist after they disappear from view. But her searches are limited; she only searches for objects where they usually disappear, not always where they are viewed to disappear.

Concept of Causality

During Stage 4 the child for the first time shows awareness that objects (besides himself) can cause activity. Up until this time, the child typically considers his own actions as the source of all causality. This change in the concept of causality is illustrated by Piaget (1954):

0;8(7) . . . (Laurent) . . . A moment later I lower my hand very slowly, starting very high up and directing it toward his feet, finally tickling him for a moment. He bursts out laughing. When I stop midway, he grasps my hand or arm and pushes it toward his feet . . .

. . . At 0;9(0) he grasps my hand and places it against his belly which I have just tickled . . .

. . . At 0;9(13) Laurent is in his baby swing which I shake three or four times by pulling a cord; he grasps my hand and presses it against the cord [p. 261].

Piaget (*The Origins of Intelligence in Children*, 1952) comments:

. . . the cause of a certain phenomenon is no longer identified by the child with the feeling he has of acting upon this phenomenon. The subject begins to discover that a spatial contact exists between cause and effect and so any object at all can be a source of activity (and not only his own body) [p. 212].

For the first time, there is an elementary externalization of causality. The child is aware that objects can be the causes of actions.

STAGE 5 (12-18 MONTHS)

In the previous stages the child developed coordination between schemata for vision and touch permitting him to prolong unusual events (Stage 3), subsequently becoming able to coordinate familiar schemata in solving *new* problems (Stage 4). In Stage 5 the child attains a higher level of operation when he begins to form *new* schemata to solve new problems. The child develops *new* means to ends through "experimentation" rather than through the application of habitual, previously formed schemata. In this case both *new* schemata and *new* coordinations are present. When confronted with a problem not solvable by the use of available schemata, the child can be seen to experiment and, through a trial-and-error process, develop *new* means (schemata). This can be seen in several examples from Piaget (Ibid.):

> Observation 167.—At 1;3(12) Jacqueline throws a plush dog outside the bars of her playpen and she tries to catch it. Not succeeding, she then pushes the pen itself in the right direction! By holding onto the frame with one hand while with the other she tried to grasp the dog, she observed that the frame was mobile. She had accordingly, without wishing to do so, moved it away from the dog. She at once tried to correct this movement and thus saw the pen approach its objective. These two fortuitous discoveries then led her to utilize movements of the playpen and to push it at first experimentally, then systematically. There was a moment's groping, but it was short.
> At 1;3(16), on the other hand, Jacqueline right away pushes her playpen in the direction of the objects to be picked up [p. 315].

In the example, Jacqueline "experiments" with playpen moving. The utility of this behavior evolves after much trial-and-error experimentation. With experience a *new* schema is developed (playpen moving) that results in the solution of a problem previously unsolvable to the child.

In the first half of the second year, the child spends much time "experimenting" with objects as in the example above. In the bathtub, objects are repeatedly pushed under water; things are splashed. The child typically is very intent on seeing how objects behave in *new* situations. For the first time, the child is able to adapt (accommodate) himself to unfamiliar situations by finding new means. Prior to Stage 5 behavior was primarily assimilatory in nature.

In terms of intellectual development, these new behaviors are particularly important. Piaget (Ibid.) suggests that behavior becomes intelligent when the child acquires the ability to solve new problems.

> . . . it can be said that the mechanism of empirical intelligence has been definitely formed. The child is henceforth capable of resolving new problems, even if no acquired (currently available) schema is directly utilizable for this purpose, and if the solution of these problems has not yet been found by deduction or representation, it is insured in principle in all cases due to the combined working of experimental search and the coordination of schemata [p. 265].

The child has reached a significant period in cognitive development when he becomes able to solve new sensorimotor problems. It marks the beginning of truly intelligent behavior in the child, the development of which started when reflex activities began in the young infant.

Object Concept

Around the age of 12 months the child's behavior indicates an awareness that objects continue to exist even though they cannot be seen. Prior to Stage 4 the child did not search for objects that were hidden, even though he viewed the disappearance. The rattle hidden under .the blanket was not retrieved. In Stage 4 (8-12 months) the child searches for objects that are hidden, but not always in the place where they are seen to be hidden. In this case the child was said to be unable to handle *sequential displacements*, i.e., if the rattle which is usually hidden in place A now is hidden in place B, the child searched for it in place A. In Stage 5 the child learns to account for sequential displacements; he searches for objects in the position resulting from the last visible displacement, not in a special place. When the rattle is hidden in A, it is searched for in A; when it is hidden in B, it is searched for in B.

Still the object concept is not yet fully developed. The child during Stage 5 typically is able to follow displacements if they are visible, but he remains unable to follow *invisible displacements*. The following interesting example illustrates this case:

> Observation 56.– . . . at 1;6(9), I resume the experiment but with a celluloid fish containing a rattle. I put the fish in the box and the box under the rug. There I shake it and Jacqueline hears the fish in the box. I turn the box upside down and bring it out empty. Jacqueline immediately takes possesion of the box, searches for the fish, turns the box over in all directions, looks around her, in particular looks at the rug but does not raise it.
> The next attempts yield nothing further . . .
> That evening I repeat the experiment with a little lamb.

Jacqueline herself puts the lamb in the box and when the whole thing is under the coverlet she says with me, "Coucou, lamb." When I take out the empty box she says, "Lamb, Lamb," but does not look under the coverlet.

Whenever I leave the whole thing under the coverlet she immediately searches for the box and brings out the lamb. But when I start again, using the first technique, she no longer looks under the coverlet! [Piaget, 1954, p.69].

While the abilities developed during Stage 5 permit Jacqueline to solve problems involving sequential displacements, she cannot yet solve those involving invisible displacements. This ability will not come about until she develops mental representation of objects (Stage 6).

Concept of Causality

In the previous stage the typical child demonstrates an awareness that other objects beyond himself can be a source of actions (causality). The following example illustrates the elaboration of the concept of causality in Stage 5:

At 1;3(30) Jacqueline holds in her right hand a box she cannot open. She holds it out to her mother, who pretends not to notice. Then she transfers the box from her right hand to her left, with her free hand grasps her mother's hand, opens it, and puts the box in it. The whole thing has occurred without a sound . . .

So also, during the next days, Jacqueline makes the adult intervene in the particulars of her game, whenever an object is too remote, etc.: she calls, cries, points to objects with her fingers, etc. In short, she well knows that she depends on the adult for satisfaction; the person of someone else becomes her best procedure for realization [Ibid., p. 275].

Not only does Jacqueline demonstrate an awareness that other people can effect activity, but also that other objects can. The following illustration shows this clearly:

> Observation 175.—At 1;2(30) Jacqueline is standing in a room which is not hers and examines the green wallpaper. Then she touches it gently and at once looks at her fingertips. This is evidently the generalization of schemata . . . touching food (jams, etc.) and looking at her fingers . . .
>
> At 1;3(12) she is standing in her playpen and I place a clown, which she recently received, on the top of the frame, in different places in sequence. Jacqueline advances laboriously along the frame but, when she arrives in front of the clown, she grasps it very cautiously and delicately, knowing that it will fall at the slightest shake. She behaved in this way ever since the first attempt. . . . Jacqueline foresees certain properties of the object which are independent of its action with respect to herself. The green wallpaper is conceived as though it ought to leave colored traces, . . . and the clown as falling down at the first touch [Piaget, *The Origins of Intelligence in Children*, 1952, pp. 327-328].

In these examples Jacqueline clearly sees objects (wallpaper, clown) as the causes of possible phenomena that are external to her actions. Prevision is seen that is *not* based on sequences of actions already observed in the same form (the wallpaper and doll are new to Jacqueline). Thus objects beyond the self are for the first time seen as causes of actions.

STAGE 6 (18-24 MONTHS)

During Stage 6 the child moves from the sensori-motor level of intelligence to representational intelligence. That is, the child becomes able to internally (mentally) represent objects and subsequently becomes able to solve problems through representation (cognitively). In Stage 5, new means for solutions to problems were attained through active experimentation. In Stage 6 the child develops new means also, but there is no appearance of experimentation as in the previous stage. Invention of means is arrived at by trying out action sequences in the head (thinking) rather than in active experimentation. In effect, the experimentation is done in thought (through representation of actions) rather than through movement. The following example illustrates Stage 6 invention of means, through representation and mental activity:

> Observation 181.—At 1;6(23) for the first time Lucienne plays with a doll carriage whose handle comes to the height of her face. She rolls it over the carpet by pushing it. When she comes against a wall, she pulls, walking backward. But as this position is not convenient for her, she pauses and without hesitation, goes to the other side to push the carriage again. She therefore found the procedure in one attempt, apparently through analogy to other situations but without training, apprenticeship, or chance.
>
> In the same kind of inventions, that is to say, in the realm of kinematic[3] representations, the following fact should be cited. At 1;10(27) Lucienne tries to kneel before a stool, but, by leaning against it, pushes it further away. She then raises herself up, takes it and places it against a sofa. When it is firmly set there she leans against it and kneels without difficulty [Ibid., p. 338].

Lucienne, in these examples, demonstrates the sudden invention of a solution to sensori-motor problems along with an awareness of causality. The suddenness of the inventions and the lack of overt experimentation suggest that the solutions are arrived at internally through mental combinations, independent of immediate experiences. Piaget explains:

> . . . instead of being controlled at each of these stages and *a posteriori* by the facts themselves, the searching is controlled *a priori* by mental combination. Before trying them, the child

---

[3] The science of motions considered apart from their causes and as applied to mechanical contrivances.

foresees which maneuvers will fail and which will succeed . . . Moreover, the procedure conceived as being capable of succeeding is in itself new, that is to say, it results from an original mental combination and not from a combination of movements actually executed at each stage of the operation [Ibid., pp. 340-341].

Thus the child becomes able to solve problems internally. For about two years this ability has been gradually evolving from sensori-motor behaviors. At this stage the child can arrive at solutions to simple motor problems without the aid of sensori-motor experimentation or the assistance of concurrent experiences.

Object Concept

The ability of the Stage 6 child to internally represent events is reflected in the child's object concept. Representation allows the child to find objects that are hidden by invisible displacement. That is, the child cannot only find objects where they are visibly hidden, but representation permits the child to search for, and find, objects that he does not see hidden. This amounts to a measure of liberation from immediate perceptions. The child knows objects are permanent. The following observation of Jacqueline demonstrates this awareness:

Observation 64.—At 1;7(20) Jacqueline watches me when I put a coin in my hand, then put my hand under a coverlet. I withdraw my hand closed; Jacqueline opens it, then searches under the coverlet until she finds the object. I take back the coin at once, put it in my hand and then slip my closed hand under a cushion situated at the other side (on her left and no longer on her right); Jacqueline immediately searches for the object under the cushion. I repeat the experiment by hiding the coin under a jacket; Jacqueline finds it without hesitation.

II. I complicate the test as follows: I place the coin in my

hand, then my hand under the cushion. I bring it forth closed
and immediately hide it under the coverlet. Finally I withdraw
it and hold it out, closed, to Jacqueline. Jacqueline then pushes
my hand aside without opening it (she guesses that there is
nothing in it, which is new), she looks under the cushion,
then directly under the coverlet where she finds the object . . .

I then try a series of three displacements: I put the coin in
my hand and move my closed hand sequentially from A to B
and from B to C; Jacqueline sets my hand aside, then searches
in A, in B and finally in C.

Lucienne is successful in the same tests at 1;3(14) [Piaget,
1954, p. 79].

The ability of the child to maintain "images" of objects
(representation) when they are absent is clearly seen in the
above example. The displacement of objects results in a
search on the part of the child until they are found.

Concept of Causality

As with the object concept and other development, the
child's awareness of causality is greatly enhanced by his
new ability to internally represent objects. Through
Stage 5 the child remains unable to predict true cause-
effect relationships in his sensori-motor world. Piaget
writes (1954):

Just as during the sensorimotor development of objects and
the spatial field the child becomes capable of evoking absent
objects and of representing to himself displacements not given
as such in the perceptual field, so also at the sixth stage the
child becomes capable of reconstructing causes in the presence
of their effects alone, and without having perceived the action
of those causes. Inversely, given a certain perceived object as
the source of potential actions, he becomes capable of foresee-
ing and representing to himself its future effects [p. 293].

The following example demonstrates Laurent's concept

of causality at this stage. Clearly through representation he accurately predicts a cause and effect relationship.

> At 1;4(4) . . . Laurent tries to open a garden gate but cannot push it forward because it is held back by a piece of furniture. He cannot account either visually or by any sound for the cause that prevents the gate from opening, but after having tried to force it he suddenly seems to understand; he goes around the wall, arrives at the other side of the gate, moves the armchair which holds it firm, and opens it with a triumphant expression [Ibid., p. 296].

Again, the rapid invention of solution to problems is seen. Such solutions were not seen in behaviors prior to Stage 6. From Laurent's actions we can infer representation of objects, a clear object concept, and a clear understanding of causality in a sensori-motor problem. Piaget (Ibid.) writes:

> In a general way, therefore, at the sixth stage the child is now capable of causal deduction and is no longer restricted to perception or sensorimotor utilization of the relations of cause to effect [p. 297].

SUMMARY OF THE
SENSORI-MOTOR PERIOD OF DEVELOPMENT

The child at age 2 is cognitively different from the infant at birth. This chapter has presented Piaget's conceptualization of how this transformation takes place. The child at birth performs only reflex activity. Toward the second month of life, the infant makes primitive differentiations of objects in its immediate environment, primarily via the sucking reflex. Between the fourth and eighth months, coordination of vision and touch typically occurs for the first time. The child grasps what it sees (Stage 3). Toward the end of the first year the child begins to develop object permanence and an awareness that objects besides himself can cause events. Two familiar schemata are coordinated to solve new problems (Stage 4). Early in the second year, true intelligent behavior typically occurs; the child evolves *new* means to solving problems through "experimentation." Also he sees himself as an object among objects (Stage 5). Toward the end of the second year, the child becomes able to internally represent objects. This ability liberates him from sensori-motor intelligence, permitting the invention of *new* means to solve problems through mental activity.

The cognitive development of the sensori-motor period evolves as the child *acts* on the environment. The actions of the child are *spontaneous* actions. The motivation for particular actions is internal. The adapting and organizing of assimilation and accommodation operate from the beginning, resulting in the continuous qualitative and quantitative change in schemata. Each new stage is characterized by behaviors reflecting qualitatively superior cognitive structures. Thus in the development of intelligence during the first two years of life, it can be seen that each new stage of development incorporates previous stages. The new stages do not displace the old, they merely improve upon them. In the same way, each stage of development helps to explain stages that follow. So it is throughout the course of cognitive development.

As the infant develops cognitively, there is a concurrent and related development of *all* concepts. Concepts do not develop independent of one another. For example, in Stage 4 (8-12 months), the typical child for the first time becomes able to systematically turn a bottle around so he can get the nipple. What does this imply about the child's concepts or schemata? First of all, the behavior suggests the child is aware of the constancy of shape of objects. Objects do not change in shape when perspectives on them change (object concept). Since all actions occur in space, the child must also have a functional concept of space and the relationships between objects. Also, the behavior of turning the bottle around is clearly an *intentional* act requiring a measure of hand-eye *coordination*. Each of these abilities evolves at about the same time. Their paths of development are one. As the child assimilates and accommodates, all his schemata are elaborated. Thus it is that evolving behaviors reflect qualitative changes in many schemata.

Upon completing the development of the sensori-motor period (it can be before or after age 2), the child has reached a point of conceptual development that is necessary for the development of spoken language and other cognitive skills during the next major period in cognitive development: the preoperational period. From this point on, the child's intellectual development will take place increasingly in the conceptual-symbolic area rather than exclusively in the sensori-motor area. This does not imply that sensori-motor development ends, only that intellectual development is to be affected by representational and symbolic activity rather than by motor activity alone.

Chapter Four

The Period of
Preoperational Thought

During the preoperational period (ages 2 to 7 years) the child evolves from one who functions primarily in a sensori-motor mode to one who functions increasingly in a conceptual and representational mode. The child becomes increasingly able to internally represent events (think) and becomes less dependent on his current sensori-motor actions for direction of behavior.

Between the ages of 2 and 7 the child's thought is characterized by new emerging abilities. Several of the most important characteristics of preoperational thought will be discussed. The development of language and the socialization of behavior will be presented first. This will be followed by a discussion of characteristics of thought that, while necessary, prevent the preoperational child from attaining completely logical, or "adult-like" thought. These are egocentrism, centration, irreversibility, and inability to follow transformations.

LANGUAGE

The single most evident development during the preoperational period is the development of spoken language. Around 2 years of age (give or take a few months), the typical child begins to use spoken words as symbols in place of objects. A word comes to represent an object. Initially the child uses "one-word" sentences, but his language facility expands quickly. By the age of 4 the typical child has largely mastered the use of spoken language. He can speak and use most grammatical rules, and he can understand what he hears if it contains familiar vocabulary. The rapid development of this form of symbolic representation (spoken language) is instrumental in facilitating the rapid conceptual development that takes place during this period.

The acquisition of language profoundly affects intellectual life. Piaget (1968) writes:

> This [language] has three consequences essential to mental development: (1) the possibility of verbal exchange with other persons, which heralds the onset of the socialization of action; (2) the internalization of words, i.e., the appearance of thought itself, supported by internal language and a system of signs; (3) last and most important, the internalization of action of such which from now on, rather than being purely perceptual and motor as it has been heretofore, can represent itself intuitively by means of pictures and "mental experiments" [p. 17].

Spoken language (and other forms of representation[1]) opens doors to the child that were not open before. The internalization of behavior through representation, facilitated by language, acts to "speed up" the rate at which experience can take place. During the sensori-motor period, "experience" could take place only as rapidly as move-

---

[1] Forms of representation other than spoken language that preoperational children use and comprehend include drawings, some symbols, and pictures and their internal "images." Use and comprehension of some written forms of representation, such as letters, written words, and numbers, develop later.

ment could occur. The child, in effect, had to carry out actions in order to "think." (Movement produced "thought.") With the development of representational skills during the preoperational period, thinking can occur in part through representations of actions rather than through actions alone. Representational thought is carried out more rapidly than thought through movement because the former is not tied to direct experience.

Piaget (1926) suggests, on the basis of his observations of young children's conversations, that there are essentially two different classifications of the preoperational child's speech: (1) egocentric speech, and (2) socialized speech. Egocentric speech is characterized by a lack of real communication. Socialized speech, on the other hand, is characterized by communication. From the ages of 2 to 4 or 5, the child's speech is largely lacking in communicative intent. He speaks in the presence of others, but without any apparent intention that others should hear his words. Even though the child speaks with others, there is no communication. Nonconversations of this type Piaget calls *collective monologues*. Speech of this type is clearly egocentric. The following example from Piaget (Ibid) demonstrates the non-communicative egocentric speech of the early preoperational child:

> Mlle. L. tells a group of children that owls cannot see by day.
> Lev: "Well, I know quite well that it can't."
> Lev (at a table where a group is at work): "I've already done moon so I'll have to change it."
> Lev picks up some barley sugar crumbs: "I say, I've got a lovely pile of eye-glasses."
> Lev: "I say, I've got a gun to kill him with. I say, I am the captain on horseback. I say, I've got a horse and a gun as well" [p. 41].

These examples of speech are clearly egocentric. Lev is

simply thinking out his actions aloud, with no desire to give anyone any information. He is having a conversation with himself in the presence of others (collective monologue).

By the ages of 6 or 7 years, language has become intercommunicative. Children's conversations clearly involve an exchange of ideas. In the following example, Lev, now considerably older than in the previous example, communicates with others in his conversations:

> Pie (6;5): "Now, you shan't have it [the pencil] because you asked for it.—" Hei (6;0): "Yes I will, because it's mine.—" Pie: "Course it isn't yours. It belongs to everybody, to all the children." —Lev (6;0): "Yes, it belongs to Mlle. L. and all the children. . ." Pie: "It belongs to Mlle. L. because she bought it, and it belongs to all the children as well" [Ibid., p. 88] .

Clearly, the above illustration involves communication. Lev in the earlier example spoke only to himself. In the last he spoke to others and clearly intended them to hear.

The development of language during the preoperational period is seen by Piaget as a gradual transition from egocentric speech characterized by *collective monologue* to socialized intercommunicative speech.

LANGUAGE AND THOUGHT

The relationship between language and thought is an important one. Piaget's formulation of sensori-motor development demonstrates that the rudiments of intelligent behavior evolve *before* language develops. Regarding the relationship between intelligence and language, Piaget (1967) writes:

> Intelligence actually appears well before language, that is to say, well before internal thought, which presupposes the use of verbal signs (internalized language). It is an entirely practical intelligence based on the manipulation of objects; in place of

words and concepts it uses percepts and movements organized into "action schema." For example, to grab a stick in order to draw up a remote object is an act of intelligence (and a fairly late developing one at that: about eighteen months). Here, an instrument, the means to an end, is coordinated with a pre-established goal...Many other examples could be cited [p. 11].

Piaget contends that the emergence of internal representation (of which spoken language is one form) increases the powers of thought in range and speed. He suggests that there are three major differences between representational and sensori-motor behavior: (1) The sequence of events in sensori-motor patterns is restricted to the speed of sensori-motor acts, making sensori-motor intelligence very slow. On the other hand, verbal behavior permits the representation of many actions very quickly. (2) Sensori-motor adaptations are limited to the immediate actions of the child, while language permits thought and adaptation to range beyond present activity. (3) Sensori-motor intelligence proceeds in a one-step-at-a-time fashion, while representational thought and language permit the child to simultaneously handle many elements in an organized manner (Piaget and Inhelder, 1969, p. 86).

Thus, because language is a form of representation of objects and events, thought involving language is liberated from the limitations of the direct action of sensori-motor thought. Cognitive activity can proceed rapidly and with a range and speed not previously available.

Another important question is whether language (in a simplistic sense) determines logical thought or whether thought determines language. Every language has a logical structure that is a socially elaborated system for relationships, classifications, and so on. The child does not "invent" language or the logic of language. Does this mean that the logic of language is the source of all the logic of the child, or does the child invent and create his own logic? Piaget and Inhelder (Ibid) cite two types of studies that support their contention that language is neither a necessary nor sufficient condition to ensure the development of logical thought. Studies of deaf mutes (no verbal language) show that they develop logical thought in the same sequential stages as normal children, but with a 1 to 2 year delay in some operations (p. 88). This suggests that language is not necessary for the development of logical operations though it clearly acts as a facilitator. Other studies of blind children, with normal verbal development, demonstrate longer delays, up to four years on the same tasks (p. 88). Blind children are hindered from birth in the development of sensori-motor schemata, and normal verbal performance does not compensate for this.

For Piaget the development of language is based on the prior development of sensori-motor operations. Thus, it is the development of sensori-motor operations that are necessary for language development, and not the other way around. When language develops there is a parallel development of conceptual abilities that language helps to facilitate, probably because language and representation permit conceptual activity to proceed more rapidly than sensori-motor operations do. The development of sensori-motor schemata is seen as a prerequisite to language development (as in blind children). Language development is seen as a facilitator of cognitive development (as in deaf children) but not as a prerequisite nor as necessary for cognitive development.

The development of physical and mathematical knowledge rests on the activity of the child. Children construct knowledge out of spontaneous actions. Language does not play any direct role in the construction of physical and logical-mathematical knowledge. In the construction of social-arbitrary knowledge, the role of spoken language is primarily one of providing an efficient means of *communi-*

cation between the child and others. This helps to make social experience more accessible to the child.

SOCIALIZATION OF BEHAVIOR

Behavior is considered social when it involves clear interchanges of ideas between people. The process of socialization begins long before behavior is social. Socialization can be traced back to the latter part of the first year of life when the child first begins to imitate other people. The process of imitation (a type of accommodation) develops until the child shows deferred imitation (imitation of absent objects) around age 2. During the preoperational period, socialization of the child's behavior can be seen in several types of activities including children's verbal exchanges and their play in games with rules (Piaget and Inhelder, 1969, p. 119).

The discussion of language pointed out that during the early part of the preoperational period, children's verbal interactions are primarily composed of collective monologue conversations. Children usually speak in the presence of others as if they are speaking to themselves. They do not ask questions or exchange information most of the time. Verbal behavior is not very communicative and not truly social. Not until ages 6 to 7 does most of children's verbal behavior become clearly communicative and social.

Games with rules also reflect children's social development. In games with rules, such as marbles, the rules are passed on from generation to generation without alteration. The young child (4 to 5 years) does not understand rules and consequently plays marbles as he understands the game. He plays as if by himself. Everybody can win. There is no collective rule to guide behavior. Around the age of 7 or 8, children become concerned with winning and with rules. Cooperation appears in these games for the first time. There is a common awareness and observance of rules and all players make sure the rules are followed. These behaviors are clearly social (Piaget, 1932).

Although Piaget has primarily investigated cognitive or intellectual development, he has indicated throughout his work his belief that all forms of development (cognitive, social, moral, etc.) evolve in an interrelated and parallel way. Intellectual and social developments do not evolve on separate schedules. Reasoning and knowledge impose constraints on the level of social reasoning a child can develop. The typical preoperational child has not constructed an adult-like schemata of *intentionality*. Consequently, there is no emergence of, nor appreciation for, social concepts like *honesty, cheating*, and *accident*. These social and moral concepts evolve in the same way that related intellectual constructions do (Kohlberg, 1976; Hersh et al., 1979).

OBSTACLES TO THE DEVELOPMENT OF LOGICAL THOUGHT

Piaget suggests that there are three levels of relationship between the actions of the child and his thought. The first is the sensori-motor level of direct action upon the environment. Between birth and age 2 all schemata are sensori-motor and dependent on the actions of the child. And the third, after age 7 or 8, is the level of operations or logical thought. The child becomes able to reason in a way that is not dependent on immediate perceptual and motor actions (period of concrete operations). Between the two, ages 2 to 7, is the preoperational period (the second level), which is an advance over sensori-motor intelligence, but is not as advanced as the logical operations of later periods. Cognitive behavior is still influenced by perceptual activities. Actions are internalized via representational functions, but thought is not liberated from perception (Piaget and Inhelder, 1969, p. 93).

The following characteristics of preoperational thought are necessary for continuous development. In addition, they serve as obstacles to logical thought. The "obstacles" to logical thought that are presented are: egocentrism, transformations, centration, and reversibility.

Egocentrism

Piaget characterizes the preoperational child's behavior and thinking as *egocentric*. That is, the child cannot take the role of or see the viewpoint of another. He believes that everyone thinks the same way he does, and that everyone thinks the same things he does. As a result, the child never questions his own thoughts because they are, as far as he is concerned, the only thoughts possible and consequently must be correct.

The preoperational child does not reflect on his own thoughts. As a result, he is never motivated to question his thinking, even when he is confronted with evidence that is contradictory to his thoughts. In such cases, the egocentric child concludes the evidence must be wrong, because his thoughts are correct. Thus, the child's thinking, from his point of view, is always quite logical and correct.

This egocentrism of thought is not egocentric by intent. The child remains unaware that he is egocentric and consequently never seeks to resolve it. Egocentrism is manifest in all the behavior of the preoperational child. As stated before, the 2- to 6-year-old's language and social behavior are largely egocentric. The child talks to himself when in the presence of others (in collective monologues) and frequently does not listen to others. Verbal behavior involves very little exchange of information and is non-social for the most part.

It is not until around the age of 6 or 7 when children's thoughts and those of their peers clearly conflict, that children begin to accommodate to others and egocentric thought begins to give way to social pressure. Peer group social interaction, the repeated conflict of one's own thoughts with those of others, eventually jars the child to question and seek verification of his thoughts. The very source of conflict, social interaction, becomes the child's source of verification. To be sure, verification of one's thoughts only comes about through comparison with the thoughts of others. Thus, peer group social interaction is the primary factor that acts to dissolve cognitive egocentrism.

While egocentrism pervades the behavior of the preoperational child, it should not be thought that egocentric behavior does not occur in other periods of development. The sensori-motor child is totally egocentric at birth (in a sensori-motor sense: unable to differentiate himself from other objects), and continues to be so throughout most of the first two years of life. Indeed, egocentrism is a characteristic of thought that is *always* present during the initial attainment and use of any new cognitive structure (schema). Later it will be seen that the adolescent, upon developing completely logical thought (formal operations), is very egocentric in his use of the newly acquired structures. Like other cognitive characteristics, egocentrism is not at a constant level throughout the period. The child from 2 to 4 is much more consistently egocentric than the child from 6 to 7. As development proceeds, egocentrism slowly wanes until it is revived when new cognitive structures are attained. Thus, egocentrism is a characteristic that pervades thought in some way in all periods of development.

Egocentric thinking, while a necessary characteristic of preoperational thought, in a sense acts to restrict the development of intellectual structures during the preoperational period. Because the child is never required by his own reasoning to question his thinking or validate his concepts, intellectual development is restricted at that time. Ego-centrism can be viewed as acting to inhibit the process of accommodation. Egocentrism acts to maintain the structural status quo. There is a tendency to assimilate rather than accommodate. Because the child does not question his own thinking, schemata are less likely to change through accommodation. While egocentrism in one sense limits cognitive development during the preoperational period, it is an essential and natural part of the period and of the initial use of any newly acquired cognitive characteristic.

Transformation

Another characteristic of the preoperational child's thinking is his inability to attend to transformations. The child, while observing a sequence of changes or successive states, focuses exclusively on the *elements* in the sequence, or the successive states, rather than on the *transformation* by which one state is changed to another. He does not focus on the process of transformation from an original state to a final state, but restricts his attention to each inbetween state when it occurs. He moves from a particular perceptual event to a particular perceptual event, but cannot integrate a series of events in terms of any beginning-end relationships. His thought is neither inductive nor deductive, but transductive.

If a pencil is held upright (as in Fig. 1) and allowed to fall, it passes from an original state (vertical) to a final state (horizontal), and through a series of successive states. Preoperational children, after viewing the pencil fall, typically cannot draw or otherwise reproduce the successive steps. They cannot attend to or reconstruct the transformation. They usually reproduce only the initial and final positions the pencil assumes.

A second example of the transformation problem is seen

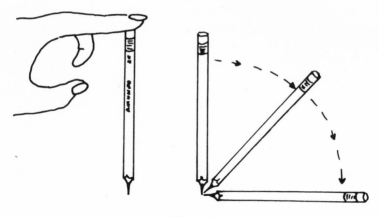

Figure 1

in a child walking through the woods. At different points he sees snails (different snails each time). The child cannot tell whether they are all the same snail or different snails. Each snail is viewed in isolation from the previous snails. The child cannot reconstruct the *transformation* from event to event (snail to snail).

The inability of the preoperational child to follow transformations inhibits the development of logic in thought. Since the child is not aware of the relationship between events and all this can mean, comparisons between states of events are always incomplete.

Centration

Another characteristic of preoperational thought is what Piaget calls *centration*. When the child is presented with a visual stimulus, he tends to *center* or fix his attention on a limited perceptual aspect of the stimulus. The child seems unable to "explore" all aspects of the stimulus, or *decenter* his visual inspection. As a result, the child when centering tends to assimilate only limited aspects of an event. Any cognitive activity seems to be dominated by the perceptual aspects. Perceptual evaluations dominate the cognitive evaluation (in the preoperational child), much in the same way as they did in the direct action of the sensori-motor child.

If a child is asked to compare two rows of like objects in which one row contains 9 objects and the other, a longer row, contains only 7 objects (spread farther apart), the child of 4 or 5 years will typically select the perceptually longer row as having "more" objects. This will occur even when the child "knows" cognitively that 9 is more than 7. Perceptual evaluation dominates cognitive evaluation.

The child tends to center on perceptual aspects of objects. It is only with time and experience that the child becomes able to *decenter* and evaluate perceptual events in a coordinated way with cognitions. After 6 to 7 years children reach the point where cognitions assume their proper position with respect to perceptions in thought.

Reversibility

Reversibility is the most clearly defined characteristic of intelligence according to Piaget (1963, p. 41). If thought is reversible, it can follow the line of reasoning back to where it started. A child without reversible thought is shown two equal-length rows of 8 coins each. He agrees that each row has the same number of coins. One of the rows is lengthened. The child no longer agrees that there are the same number of coins in each row. Part of the child's problem is that he is not able to *reverse* the act of lengthening. He cannot maintain the equivalence of number in the face of perceptual change in a dimension that is irrelevant to number (length). Only when actions become reversible will the child be able to solve such problems. The inability to reverse operations is seen in all cognitive activity of the preoperational child.

Preoperational thought retains much of the rigidity of sensori-motor thought even while surpassing it in quality. It is slow, plodding, inflexible, dominated by perceptions, and irreversible. The attainment of reversible operations is extremely difficult for the child. This is reasonable if one considers that *all* sensori-motor operations are irreversible by definition. Once a motor act is committed, it cannot be reversed. In much the same way perceptions cannot be reversed. Thus representational acts, which are based on prior sensori-motor patterns and perceptions, must develop reversibility without any prior patterns to follow (Ibid., p. 41).

Sensori-motor and preoperational children construct concepts and knowledge about such things as space and causality from their actions on their environment. The environment contains physical elements and orderings; when these are acted on by the child, they permit concepts to be constructed or "discovered" (physical knowledge). Certain concepts or knowledge cannot be constructed or "discovered" directly from examples in the environment but must be *invented* by the child. This is true of many logical-mathematical concepts. For example, the environment does not contain many physical examples of reversibility the child can use as models for developing reversibility of thought and reasoning. Reversibility must therefore be invented by the child.

Piaget's concepts of egocentrism, centration, transformation, and reversibility are closely related. Early preoperational thought is dominated by the presence or absence of each of them. As cognitive development proceeds, these characteristics gradually subside in unison. A deterioration in egocentrism permits (requires) the child to decenter more and attend to simple transformations. All this in turn helps the child in his construction of reversibility.

CONSERVATION

The characteristics of preoperational thought described function as obstacles to logical thought. Nonetheless they are necessary for the development of logical thought and occur naturally. They are most clearly seen in what have come to be called conservation problems. The problems described on the following pages were developed by Piaget and his co-workers to assess children's levels of conceptual development and their level of attainment with respect to the concepts involved. Conservation is the conceptualization (schematization) that the amount or quantity of a matter stays the same regardless of any changes in an irrelevant dimension. For example, if we have a row of 8 pennies, and we move the pennies farther apart in the row, we still have 8 pennies. That is, the number of pennies does not change when a change is made in another, irrelevant, dimension (in this case, the length of the row). An awareness of the number invariance would imply ability to conserve number and that corresponding schemata have developed. Lack of this awareness implies lack of number conservation, and that corresponding schemata (reversibility) have not developed. This level of conservation ability is a measure of the type of intellectual structures the child has developed. During the preoperational period, children typically cannot conserve; that is, they cannot hold one dimension invariant in the face of changes in other dimensions. By the end of the preoperational period (age 7) some conservation structures are usually developed.

The development from non-conservation to conservation is a gradual one. As with all other changes in cognitive structures (schemata), the change is largely a function of

the actions (cognitive and sensori-motor) of the child. According to Piaget, conservation structures cannot be induced through direct instruction (teaching) or reinforcement techniques. Active experience is the key. Conservation of number, area, and volume problems will be presented, followed by a discussion of some of the research
that has been done on children's concepts of conservation.

Conservation of Number

If a 4- to 5-year-old is presented with a row of checkers
and asked to construct a row that is the same, he typically
constructs a row of the same length, but his row may not
correspond in the number of elements to the model. The
typical construction proceeds by placing two checkers, one
opposite each of the end checkers in the model, and then
filling in a number of checkers without one-to-one correspondence. If there is correspondence, it is by accident
(Piaget, 1967, p. 31).

The 5- to 6-year-old is usually a little more systematic.
When he is asked to perform the same conservation task,
he uses one-to-one correspondence and makes each row
equal in number and length to the model. But, if the child
sees one row lengthened (transformed as in Fig. 2) without
any change in the number of elements, the child declares
they are no longer equivalent. This is frequently true even

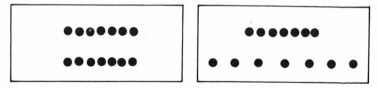

Figure 2

if he counts the elements in each row. The preoperational

child holds that the rows are equivalent only as long as there is visual correspondence in the length of arrays (Ibid., p. 31).

The typical child of 5 or 6 does not conserve number. He cannot see that number of elements in a series does not change in the face of other perceptual changes. What has happened (according to Piagetian theory) is that after a transformation the child makes a perceptual response, instead of a cognitive response. In terms of previous notions of *centration*, the child focuses or centers on one aspect of the event—the length of the rows—and ignores other salient aspects of which he is cognitively aware: the number of objects. Also, the child does not focus on the *transformation* of stimulus arrays, but focuses on each successive state as if it were independent of the previous states. Thus, the child, because of his inability to decenter and focus on the transformation, typically ends up making a perceptual response. Unable to *reverse* the changes that he has seen occur, he resorts to a perceptual response. The child is, in this respect, "perception bound." When confronted with a problem where cognitive and perceptual solutions conflict, the child makes decisions based on the perceptual cues.

Around the age of 6 or 7 the typical child learns to conserve number. Concurrently he *decenters* his perceptions, attends to the *transformations*, and *reverses* operations. He constructs an awareness that a change in the length of a row of elements (an irrelevant dimension) does not change the number of elements in the row.

Conservation of Area

A second type of conservation problem reflects the child's concepts of *area*. This can be demonstrated by the cows-in-the-field problem (Piaget, Inhelder, and Szeminska, 1960, p. 262). Two sheets of green paper (same size) are placed before the child, and a cow (toy or paper cut-out) is placed in each field, as in Figure 3a. Several blocks of the same size are kept on hand to represent buildings. It is explained to the child that there are two fields of grass and a cow in each field. The child is asked; "Which cow has more grass to eat?" Typically, the response will be that both cows have the same amount of grass to eat. Once visual equivalence of area is established, the child is shown a barn (block) being placed in each field, and the question is repeated: "Which cow has more grass to eat now?" Again, the response is typically that they both have the same amount of grass. A second block is placed in each field (Fig. 3b); but in the first field, the second block is placed away from the first, and in the other field the second block is placed adjacent to the first. The question is repeated: "Which cow has more grass to eat now?" The child who cannot conserve typically says that the cow in the second field (blocks adjacent) has more grass to eat. His reasoning suggests that the field with two adjacent barns (one set of barns) has more grass area than the field with two separated barns (two sets of barns), even though the barns are seen as the same size. The child who can conserve says that they both have the same amount to eat. The conserver clearly reasons that the placement of barns is irrelevant to area. The important thing is the number of barns. The extension of this problem by more barn placements can be varied to check the reliability of the conservation or non-conservation responses.

Again, the non-conserving preoperational child has made a perceptual response. The second field looks like it has less buildings (because they are attached) than the first field. The child is not able to *decenter* and attend to all the salient aspects of the event, nor does he follow the *transformations* that have taken place. Each new placement is independent of the previous. Thus, as with conservation of

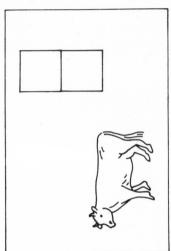

Figure 3b

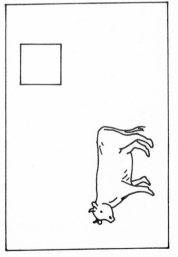

Figure 3a

number problems, the preoperational child fails to conserve. Not until ages 7 to 8 is conservation of area usually attained.

Conservation of Liquid

A third type of problem is the conservation of liquid problem. The preoperational child's inability to conserve liquid can usually be shown with the following task. The child is presented with two containers of equal size and shape, as in Figure 4. The child is asked to compare the

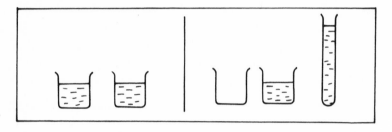

Figure 4

amount of liquid in the two containers. A few drops are added to one, if necessary, to establish visual equivalence of volume. When equivalence is attained, the liquid from one of the glasses is poured into a taller and thinner glass (or shorter and wider glass), and the child is again asked to compare the two containers holding liquid. As in the previous problems, an irrelevant dimension has been changed. The typical preoperational child no longer sees the two containers as equivalent in volume and declares that one or the other (usually the taller and thinner container) has more liquid. Reasoning is usually based on the height of one column of liquid compared with the other. This is clearly a non-conservation response. If the liquid is then poured back into the original container, visual equivalence is usually achieved again for the child, though not because the child conserves.

As in the previous conservation problems, the preoperational child typically does not attend to all aspects of the *transformation* that he sees. He *centers* on the perceptual aspects of the problem. Because the taller cylinder looks larger, it must contain more liquid. Reasoning is not logical. Reversibility is not present. It is not until concrete operations (ages 7 to 11) that liquid conservation is usually present.[2]

The preceding conservation problems illustrate but do not begin to exhaust the phenomenon of conservation. Qualitative differences in the logical thought of the child manifest themselves in *all* aspects of their thinking. A change along one irrelevant dimension always seems to imply changes in the relevant dimensions for the preoperational child. The reverse is true for his older counterparts who develop schemata permitting conservation.

The picture of conservation presented here is somewhat oversimplified. The child does not develop conservation schemata overnight in an all-or-nothing manner. Conservation concepts are acquired slowly after much experience and subsequent assimilation and accommodation. Qualitatively new patterns of responses are interpreted by Piaget to reflect newly formed schemata (cognitive structures).

The acquisition of schemata permitting conservation does not take place at the same time in all areas. The application of conservation principles to different types of problems usually follows a sequence. Conservation of num-

---

[2] Liquid problems of the above type are usually solved after 7 or 8. More sophisticated volume conservation problems, such as those requiring the measurement of displaced water when an object is immersed, are not solved until about age 12 [Piaget and Inhelder, 1969, p. 98].

ber is usually attained before other conservation skills, and conservation of volume is usually attained last. The structures permitting conservation are typically acquired at the following ages:

number	5-6
substance (mass)	7-8
area	7-8
liquid	7-8
weight	9-10
volume	11-12

Such a developmental sequence suggests that the ability to conserve volume always implies the ability to conserve weight, area, substance, and number. Each new type of conservation always implies that previous levels in the sequence have been attained.[3]

RESEARCH ON CONSERVATION LEARNING

Piaget's conceptualizations indicate that conservation concepts are acquired in a sequence. Research on the sequential development of conservation concepts is also found in the literature and these studies generally confirm Piaget's findings. Urgiris (1968) found that of 120 subjects

[3] Under the guidance of competent and trained persons, problems like the conservation problems and others can be used to assess children's intellectual development from a Piagetian point of view. They can also be used to determine a child's level of development regarding a particular concept. Many professionals feel that a Piagetian methodology provides a substitute for, or a supplement to, conventional intelligence testing because Piagetian methods *clearly* measure reasoning. logical thought, and knowledge. Competency in making valid assessments takes time and training. Those interested in learning more about how to make such assessments can consult works that deal with Piagetian assessment in detail (e.g., Wadsworth, 1978; Piaget, *The Child's Conception of the World,* 1963; Copeland, 1974).

between the ages of 7 and 11, 112 evidenced conservation of substance, weight, and volume in the order Piaget describes. Elkind (*Children's Discovery of the Conservation of Mass, Weight, and Volume, 1961*) tested 175 children in kindergarten to grade six on conservation of mass, weight, and volume. The results of his study confirmed Piaget's findings with respect to the age at which conservation concepts are attained and with respect to the order in which they are attained. Another study by Elkind (*Quality Conceptions in Junior and Senior High School Students, 1961*) involving problems in conservation of mass, weight, and volume found the sequence suggested by Piaget in 469 junior and senior high school students. These studies confirm Piaget's belief that conservation concepts are attained in an invariant sequence.

A second set of studies deals with the effects of schooling, direct instruction, and reinforcement techniques on the acquisition of conservation skills. Most of these studies suggest that direct teaching does not produce permanent conservation learning in preoperational children.

Gruen (1965) unsuccessfully used training procedures to try to induce conservation of number skills in 45 kindergarten children. Wohlwill and Lowe (1962) found that continued reinforced practice in conservation of number was ineffective in improving conservation responses. Wallach, Wall, and Anderson (1967), using 56 first-graders, examined the effect of reversibility training and addition and subtraction experience on conservation of number. No effect due to the addition and subtraction training was noted. Reversibility training was reported to affect conservation responses. Kohlberg (1968) found that a special Montessori schooling program for children over a nine-month period raised I.Q. test scores but did not significantly affect performance on conservation tasks. These studies all add credence to Piaget's belief that cognitive structures (schemata) cannot be induced directly as a substitute for general experience.

Along similar lines, a number of studies have been done on the conservation ability of children who have not had formal schooling. Unschooled children typically evolve conservation concepts at about the same age as schooled children in most cultures. Mermelstein and Schulman (1967) examined the conservation responses on a number of conservation tasks of 6- and 9-year-old black children in Prince Edward County, Virginia, who had not attended school for four years. These responses were compared with the responses on the same tasks of Northern black children who had attended school. No significant differences between the groups were found. Goodnow and Bethon (1966), in a study of Hong Kong children, similarly found no differences between the performance of unschooled and schooled children of comparable intelligence on various conservation tasks. As in other studies, all tasks showed a close relation to the mental age of children.

In contrast with the preceding studies, Greenfield (1966) found that unschooled Senegalese children from bush areas were significantly retarded in conservation ability when compared with city and bush children that had had schooling.

These few studies suggest that formal schooling, or lack of it, does not usually influence conservation ability, but that conservation abilities appear at about the same age in schooled and unschooled subjects. According to Piaget's theory, instruction (schooling) rarely leads directly to the formation of a stable schemata for conservation. Qualitative changes in schemata can come about only with considerable general active experience which children usually have regardless of whether they go to school or not. Intellectual structures (schemata) cannot be erected on demand but are contingent on a background of general experience.[4]

Piaget contends that conservation abilities evolve "naturally" out of the experiences most children have. Children tend to develop conservation abilities at about the same age, and tend to develop different conservation operations in an invariant sequence. In most cultures, children without formal schooling attain conservation as readily as

children with schooling, and direct teaching of conservation skills to preoperational children is not generally successful.

---

[4]This should not be interpreted to mean that children learn regardless of whether they go to school. It means only that cognitive structures (schemata) will evolve in most cases regardless of whether children go to school or not. Chapter Eight deals with this in more detail.

The interpretation of these findings according to Piagetian theory is that conservation abilities will not emerge until cognitive structures (schemata) evolve that make true conservation responses possible. Changes in schemata come about only after considerable assimilation and accommodation of experience. The child must attain reversibility, learn to decenter perceptions, and follow transformations. He must become less egocentric and learn to question his thinking. These changes all come about gradually and are prerequisites to the development of the schemata permitting conservation.

SUMMARY OF THE PREOPERATIONAL PERIOD

Qualitatively the thought of the preoperational child is an advance over the thought of the sensori-motor child. It is no longer primarily restricted to immediate perceptual and motor events. Thought is truly representational (symbolic) and behavior sequences can be played out in the head rather than only in real physical events. Even so, perception still dominates reasoning. When conflicts arise between perception and thought, as in the conservation problems, children using preoperational reasoning make judgments based on perception.

The preoperational period is marked by some dramatic attainments. Language is acquired very rapidly between the ages of 2 and 4. Behavior in the early part of the period is largely egocentric and non-social. These characteristics become less dominant as the period proceeds and by age 6 or 7 children's conversations become largely communicative and social.

While preoperational thought is an advance over sensori-motor thought, it is restricted in many respects. The child is unable to reverse operations, he cannot follow transformations; perceptions tend to be centered, and the child is egocentric. These characteristics make for slow, concrete, and restricted thought. During this period thought is still largely under the control of the immediate and the perceptual, as is seen in the typical preoperational child's inability to solve conservation problems.

Cognitive development is not arrested from ages 2 to 7. Rather, it moves steadily along, assimilation and accommodation resulting in the constant evolution of new and improved cognitive machinery (schemata). The preoperational child's behavior is initially like that of the sensori-motor child. By age 7 there is little resemblance.

Chapter Five

Period of Concrete Operations

During the period of concrete operations (ages 7 to 11), the child's reasoning processes become logical. He develops what Piaget calls *logical operations*. That is, the child evolves logical thought processes (operations) that can be applied to concrete problems. Unlike the preoperational child, the concrete operational child has no trouble solving the conservation problems. When faced with a discrepancy between thought and perception, as in conservation problems, the concrete operational child makes cognitive and logical decisions as opposed to perceptual decisions. The concrete operational child is no longer perception-bound. He becomes able, between the ages of 7 and 11, to do all the cognitive operations that limit the intellectual activity of the preoperational child. He *decenters* his perceptions and attends to *transformations*. Most important, the concrete operational child attains *reversibility* of operations. In addition, cooperative, nonegocentric communication evolves. The child for the first time becomes a truly social being.

The quality of concrete operational thought surpasses that of preoperational thought. Schemata for the operations of seriation and classification appear. Improved concepts of causality, space, time, and speed evolve. In essence, the concrete operational child attains a level of intellectual activity that is superior in all respects to that of the preoperational child.

While the concrete operational child evolves a functional use of logic not evidenced in the behavior of younger children, he does not attain the highest level of use of logical operations. Here the term *concrete* (as in concrete operations) is significant. While the child clearly evolves logical operations, these operations (reversibility, classification, etc.) are only useful to him in solving problems involving concrete (real, observable) objects and events. For the most part, the child cannot yet apply his logic to problems that are hypothetical, purely verbal, or abstract. If the concrete operational child is presented with a purely verbal problem, he is typically unable to solve it correctly. If the same problem is presented in terms of real objects, the child can apply his logical operations and solve the problem. Thus, the concrete operational period can be viewed as being a transition between pre-logical (preoperational) thought and the completely logical thought of the older child.

HOW CONCRETE OPERATIONAL THOUGHT DIFFERS FROM PREOPERATIONAL THOUGHT

The preoperational child's thought is characterized by dominance of perception over reasoning, egocentrism, centration, inability to follow transformations, and inability to reverse operations. These obstacles to logical thought are reflected in the preoperational child's inability to solve conservation problems. In contrast, concrete operational thought is free of all the characteristics that dominated preoperational thought. The typical concrete operational child can solve the conservation problems. His thought is less egocentric, he can decenter his perceptions, he follows transformations, and most important, he can reverse operations. When conflicts arise between perception and reasoning, the concrete operational child makes judgments based on reasoning. These characteristics will be discussed in the following pages.

Egocentrism and Socialization

The preoperational child's thinking was dominated by egocentrism, an inability to assume the viewpoint of others and a lack of a need to seek validation of his own thoughts. The concrete operational child's thinking is not egocentric in this respect. He is aware that others can come to conclusions that are different from his, and as a consequence he comes to seek validation of his thoughts. In this respect the concrete operational child is liberated from the intellectual egocentrism of the previous period.

Liberation from egocentrism, according to Piaget, comes about primarily through social interaction with peers.[1] During social (conceptual) interaction with peers, the child is forced to seek verification of his ideas. Piaget (1928) writes:

> What then gives rise to the need for verification? Surely it must be the shock of our thoughts coming into contact with that of others, which produces doubt and the desire to prove . . . The social need to share the thoughts of others and to communicate our own with success is at the root of our need for verification. Proof is the outcome of argument . . . Argument is, therefore, the backbone of verification [p. 204].

The concrete operational child does not display the ego-

---

[1] Piaget states that social interaction is one of the variables that facilitates cognitive development. His writings suggest that social interactions are any behaviors (conversations, play, games, etc.) that involve a real interchange between two or more persons. Thus, when language becomes functionally communicative, it is a form of social interaction.

centrism of thought characteristic of the preoperational child. At this time his use of language becomes communicative in function. Through social interaction concepts are verified or denied. As has been said previously, the socialization of behavior is a continuous process that begins in early childhood with simple imitations. Social behavior, by its very nature, is an important form of accommodation. Coming to look at something from another's viewpoint, questioning one's reasoning, and seeking validation from others are all essentially acts of accommodation.

The process of socialization is progressive rather than regressive (Piaget and Inhelder, 1969, p. 117). That is, the child's behavior is always becoming more social. Children's behaviors in games with rules become increasingly social. In the games of marbles, after the age of 7 or so, behaviors are well structured with common adherence to rules and a collective spirit of honest competition. Prior to 7 years, each child plays to have fun and everyone can win. True cooperation and competition (social behavior) do not appear before the concrete operations (Ibid., p. 119).

With the arrival of concrete operations, language becomes less egocentric. Collective monologues, characteristic of children's speech before 6 or 7 years, are largely absent after that time. Children exchange information with each other in their conversations and learn to speak from the viewpoint of others.

Centration

The preoperational child's thinking is characterized by centration or centering. Perceptions of events tend to center on a single perceptual characteristic of a stimulus and to not take into account all the salient features of the stimulus. Thus, in conservation of number problems, preoperational children tend to center on the length of stimulus configurations.

The concrete operational child's thinking is not characterized by centering. Concrete thought becomes *decentered*, taking into account all the salient features of objects. Decentering is one of the abilities found in concrete thought that permits logical solutions to concrete problems.

Transformations

The preoperational child was unable to coordinate and focus on the successive steps in a transformation. Each step in a transformation was viewed as independent of each successive step. There was no awareness or attention paid to the sequence or transformation involved.

The concrete operational child attains a functional understanding of transformations. He can solve problems involving transformations and is aware of and understands the relationship between successive steps.

Reversibility

Preoperational thought lacks reversibility. Concrete operational thought is reversible. The difference between the two levels of thought can be seen in the following illustra-

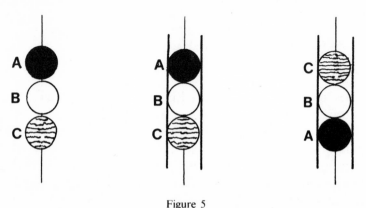

Figure 5

tion from Piaget (1967, p. 31). A child is shown three balls of the same size, each of a different color (A, B, C). The balls are placed in a cylinder in the order A, B, C. The preoperational child correctly predicts that they will exit from the bottom of the cylinder in the same order, A, B, C. Once more the balls are in the cylinder in the same order. Then the cylinder is rotated 180 degrees. The preoperational child continues to predict that the balls will exit from the bottom of the tube in the same order as before, A, B, C. He is surprised when they exit in the order C, B, A. This is an example of the inability of preoperational thought to reverse operations. The concrete operational child has no trouble with the above problem. He can reverse the inversion and make the appropriate deduction. In this way concrete thought is reversible.

Conservation

The hallmark of preoperational thought is the inability of the child to conserve. With the attainment of concrete operations, the ability to solve conservation problems emerges. The related abilities to decenter, to follow transformations, and to reverse operations are all instrumental in developing conservation skills. The child becomes able to solve the conservation of number problems around age 6 or 7. Conservation of area and mass problems are usually solved by age 7 or 8. Conservation of volume problems (measurement of displaced water when an object is immersed) are not solved correctly until age 11 or 12.

LOGICAL OPERATIONS

Cognitively, the most important development of the concrete operational period is the attainment of logical operations. Logical operations are internalized cognitive actions that permit the child to arrive at conclusions that are "logical." These actions are directed by cognitive activity rather than being dominated by perceptions. Logical operations evolve, as do all cognitive structures, out of prior structures as a function of assimilation and accommodation. Logical operations are means of organizing experience (schemata) that are superior to prior organization.

According to Piaget, an operation always has four characteristics. It is an action that can be internalized or carried out in thought as well as materially. It is reversible. An operation always supposes some conservation, some invariance. And an operation never exists alone but is always related to a system of operations (Piaget, 1970, pp. 21-22). Operations become truly logical during the concrete operational period. Previous operations (preoperational period) were pre-logical, never meeting all the above criteria. One logical operation already discussed is reversibility. Two other operations are seriation and classification.

Seriation

A cognitive operation acquired during the concrete operational period is seriation, the ability to mentally arrange elements according to increasing or decreasing size. If a

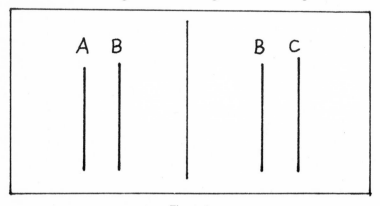

Figure 6

preoperational child (before 6 or 7 years) is shown two sticks of slightly different lengths (A and B), he can compare them and visually determine that A is shorter than B. If he is then shown sticks B and C (where B is shorter than C) while A is hidden from view, he can again visually determine that B is less than C. If the child is then asked to compare A to C, while A is still hidden, he cannot make the appropriate deduction (A < B, B < C, so A < C). The child typically requests to see A and C together so he can compare them. Such responses indicate the preoperational child cannot mentally order events in a series. He cannot construct the necessary mental scale to order objects or events.

Different kinds of seriation learning, like conservation learning, typically occur at different ages in an invariant sequence. The child first learns to seriate length (as in the above problem) around age 7, the beginning of concrete operations. Seriation of weight (seriation of objects of the same size but different weight) is usually attained around age 9. Similarly, seriation of volume is not arrived at until age 12 or so (Piaget, 1967, p. 51). As can be seen, the ability to seriate or order objects or events along a particular dimension (length, weight, volume), occurs at about the same time as conservation skills emerge with respect to the same dimension.

In a manner analogous to the development of seriation concepts, the child develops concepts of equivalence (A = B; B = C; therefore A = C). Length, weight, and volume equivalences are attained at about the same time as concepts of seriation and conservation with respect to each dimension. Equivalence of length is attained before equivalence of volume (Ibid., p. 51).

Classification

Classification is another logical operation that becomes

operative during the concrete operational period. Prior to that period children have certain problems in classifying objects and events and relating these classifications. The following example from Piaget (*The Child's Conception of Number*, 1952) illustrates the development of operations involved in the comparison of classes. A child is shown a box containing 20 wooden beads, 18 of which are brown; the other 2 white. The child is told to examine the beads and put the brown beads in a separate box. When this is properly accomplished, it indicates the child has the classification "brown." The same procedure is used to establish

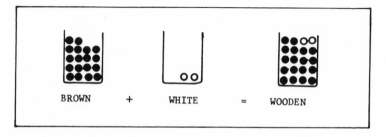

Figure 7

the child's ability to classify according to "white" and "wooden." Most children can make these simple classifications by age 4. Once the classes of brown, white, and wooden have been established, the child is asked, "Are there more wooden beads or more brown beads?" They are also asked for the reasoning behind their answers.

At the preoperational level most children respond that there are more brown beads than wooden beads. At the concrete operational level (after age 7), most children respond that there are more wooden beads than brown beads. The preoperational child cannot perform the *logical operation* of the addition of classes, while the concrete operational child can. The concrete operational child can simultaneously take into consideration two kinds of classes. He can perform the addition of classes and he can reverse the process. After age 8 or so the typical child understands the relationship between an included class (subclass) and an entire class. The preoperational child seems to be able to classify the beads along only one dimension at a time. He cannot compare the beads as both wooden and white, or both wooden and brown. An apparent perceptual difference exists between the beads in the problem, and the preoperational child makes a perceptual response. As in conservation problems, the preoperational child *centers* on one dimension (color) and is unable to consider at the same time the common wooden characteristics of all the beads.

A number of experimenters have studied the development of classification behaviors in children. Kofsky (1966) did an analysis of eleven different classification tasks with children from ages 4 to 9. These tasks were all derived from Piaget's work. The observed order of task difficulty reported by Kofsky was in accord with the theoretical expectations derived from Piaget's work. A significant correlation between the ages of the children studied and the number of tasks they completed successfully was found ($r = .86$, $p. < .01$). Ability to perform classifications was related to age. These results tend to confirm Piaget's notions with respect to classifications. Kofsky also conducted an analysis (scalogram) of the sequence in which classifications theoretically were expected to occur. The results of the analysis were partially confirming. Some children passed theoretically difficult tasks while not being able to pass easier tasks.

By now it should be clear to the reader that Piaget conceptualizes cognitive development as occurring not in isolation, but in all areas at the same time. A cognitive advance in one area has effects in other areas. With this in mind, the concrete operational child's concepts of causality, time, and speed will be discussed.

Causality

Children's concepts of causality develop as do other concepts. Development of causal concepts during the sensorimotor period was illustrated in Chapter Three. Piaget and Inhelder (1969) investigated children's concepts of causality in the following problem situation:

> . . . we once asked children from five to twelve what happens after lumps of sugar are dissolved in a glass of water. For children up to about seven, the dissolved sugar disappears and its taste vanishes like a mere odor; for children seven to eight its substance is retained without either its weight or its volume. After nine or ten, conservation of weight is present, and after eleven or twelve, there is also conservation of volume (recognizable in the fact that the level of water, which is slightly raised when the sugar is added, does not return to its initial level after the sugar is dissolved) [p. 112].

As illustrated in the above example, children's causal concepts develop during the concrete operational period. Qualitative changes in structures (schemata) are reflected in the development.

Time and Speed

Piaget contends that children do not understand the relationship between time and speed (velocity = speed/time) until age 10 or 11 (Piaget and Inhelder, 1969, p. 103). Prior to this age an object is considered to travel faster than another object only if it overtakes it while moving. The preoperational child, when comparing the speeds of two objects, usually considers only the points of arrival, and does not consider starting points and subsequent velocity or paths followed (Ibid., p. 108). Consider the following example. Two cars leave point A in Figure 8 at the same time. They both arrive at B at the same time but traverse different routes (1 and 2). After viewing this problem, observing the movement of the cars, the preoperational child reports both cars traveled at the same speed. It is not until after age 8 or so, according to Piaget, that a ratio concept of speed in terms of the relationship between time and distance traveled begins to evolve.

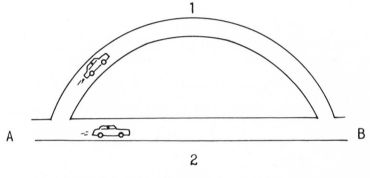

Figure 8

The concrete operational child's concepts of time and speed are superior to those of the preoperational child. Not until the period of concrete operations do reliable concepts appear.

SUMMARY OF THE PERIOD OF CONCRETE OPERATIONS

The period of concrete operations can be viewed as a transition period between preoperational thought and formal (logical) thought. During this period the child attains the use of logical operations for the first time. Thought is no longer dominated by perceptions, the child being able to logically solve concrete problems.

The concrete operational child is not egocentric in his thought. He can assume the viewpoints of others and his language is social and communicative. He can decenter his perceptions and attend to transformations. All these new characteristics of thought are reflected in his ability to solve the conservation problems that he was previously unable to solve. An important attainment is reversibility, an essential quality in all operations. Two operations developed during this period are seriation and classification.

While concrete thought is clearly superior to preoperational thought, it remains inferior to the thought of the older child (over 11 or 12). The concrete operational child can use logical operations to solve problems involving "concrete" objects and events. He cannot solve hypothetical problems, problems that are entirely verbal, and some problems requiring more complex or "abstract" operations. Only with the attainment of formal thought will the development of cognitive structures be complete.

Chapter Six

The Period of Formal Operations

During the period of formal operations, approximately ages 11 to 15 years or older, the child develops the reasoning and logic to solve all classes of problems. According to Piaget, the child's cognitive structures reach maturity during this period. That is, his potential in terms of quality of thought (compared with the potential of "adult" thought) is at its maximum *when* formal operations are achieved. After this period there are no further structural improvements in the quality of reasoning one is capable of. The adolescent with formal operations typically has the cognitive *structural* equipment to think "as well as" adults. This does not mean that adolescent (formal) thought is necessarily "as good as" adult thought in a particular instance, only that the attainment of formal operations means a new potentiality has been achieved.

Assimilation and accommodation continue throughout life to produce changes in schemata. From the end of the period of formal operations, changes in thought abilities are quantitative and no longer qualitative with respect to logical operations and structure. Quality of reasoning does not improve after this period. Content and function of intelligence may improve. This is not meant to imply that the use of thought cannot or does not improve after adolescence. The content and function (use to which thought is put) of thought are free to vary and improve after this period, which in part helps to explain some of the classical differences between adolescent thought and adult thought (see Chapter Seven).

One should not assume that all adolescents and adults fully develop formal operations. Studies by Elkind (1962), Kohlberg and Mayer (1972), Schwebel (1975), and Kuhn et al. (1977) have shown that no more than half the American population may develop all the possibilities of formal operations. Certainly a large proportion of the American adult population never advances much beyond concrete operational reasoning.

HOW FORMAL OPERATIONS DIFFER FROM CONCRETE OPERATIONS

Functionally, formal thought and concrete thought are the same. They both employ logical operations. The major difference between the two types of thought is the much larger range of application of logical operations available to the child with formal thought. Concrete thought is limited to solving tangible concrete problems of the present. Concrete operational children cannot deal with complex verbal problems, hypothetical problems, or those involving the future. To this extent, the concrete operational child is not completely free of his perceptions. In contrast, the child with fully developed formal operations can deal with all classes of problems, the present, past, and future, the hypothetical, and the verbal. Thus, the child with formal operations is liberated from concrete problems. During this period the child becomes capable of introspection; he is able to think about his own thoughts and feelings as if they were objects.

The concrete operational child must deal with each problem in isolation. Operations are not coordinated. The child cannot integrate his solutions by means of general theories. The child with formal operations can employ theories in the solution of many problems in an integrated manner. Several operations can be brought to bear on a single problem.

In addition, formal operations are characterized by scientific reasoning, hypothesis building (and testing), and they reflect a true understanding of causation. For the first time the child can operate on the logic of an argument (problem) independent of its content. He is aware that logically derived conclusions have a validity independent of factual truth. While both concrete thought and formal thought have much in common, they are clearly different. The concrete operational child lacks the range and power of thought of his older counterpart.

CHARACTERISTICS OF FORMAL OPERATIONS

Formal thought and reasoning arise out of concrete operations in the same way that each new level of thought incorporates and modifies prior thought. During the period of formal operations the child is better able to organize data, reason scientifically, and generate hypotheses. These characteristics of thought are seen in a number of problems easily solved with formal operations but impossible to solve with concrete operations. Such problems are those involving inverses of reciprocals, combinatorial thought, complex verbal problems, hypothetical problems, proportions, and conservation of movement. Examples of each of these are presented next.

Combinatorial Thought

Piaget and Inhelder (1969) describe the difference between concrete and formal thought in a problem involving combinatorial thought. A child is presented with five jars containing colorless liquids. The combination of three of the liquids (1, 3, 5) produces a yellow color. One of the other two jars contains a bleaching agent and one water. The child is shown the colored liquid that can be produced but he does not see how it is obtained. When children are asked to produce the yellow color, those of 7 to 11 years typically proceed by combining two liquids at a time. After combining pairs, the systematic nature of their searching stops. They may then mix all five together (which does not produce a yellow color). After the age of 12 children typically test all possible combinations of two and three liquids until the yellow solution is reached (Piaget and Inhelder, 1969, p. 134).

The concrete operational child's explorations are systematic up to a certain point, but he does not explore all possible combinations. In contrast, the child with formal operations explores all the logically possible solutions. Again, the qualitative difference between concrete and formal thought is illustrated.

Verbal Problems

Children without formal operations are usually not able to solve the following verbal problem. The problem is derived from one of Burt's tests that was standardized by Piaget early in his career.

> Edith is fairer than Susan; Edith is darker than Lilly; Who is the darkest of the three? (Piaget, 1968, p. 162).

Children under the age of 12 have trouble solving this problem. Their reasoning is similar to that of the younger child in the previous problem of serializing sticks. Not until age 12 or later can children usually do with verbal problems what they learned to do with concrete problems around age 7 (Ibid., p. 149).

Hypothetical Problems

The child with formal operations can reason on the basis of assumption while children with concrete thought cannot. The older child can operate on the logic of an argument independently of its content. He is aware that conclusions logically derived from assumptions have a validity that is independent of their factual truth.

If a logical argument is prefixed by the statement, "Suppose coal is white . . .,"[1] the concrete operational child, when asked to solve the logical problem, declares that coal is black and that he cannot answer the question. Presented with the same problem, the child with formal operations readily accepts the assumption that coal is white and proceeds with the logic of the argument. The older child can extract the structure of the argument from its content and submit the structure (alone) to logical analysis. The concrete operational child typically cannot deal with an argument independent of its content. Coal is black and the problem is unsolvable.

Inverse of Reciprocals

Concrete operational children understand the reasoning involved in reciprocals. For example, if Bill is older than Sam, then it follows that Sam is younger than Bill. Here, older and younger are reciprocals of each other. In general, concrete reasoning can be applied to reciprocals, and so the concrete operational child has little difficulty reasoning about them.

The *inverse* of a reciprocal is much further removed from concrete experience and borders on the hypothetical. Reasoning accurately about the inverse of reciprocals does not occur until early formal operations. A child is told to as-

---

[1] Adapted from Elkind (1967).

sume that *if a woman is blond, she is pretty.* The child is subsequently asked two questions involving inverses of reciprocals: (1) *If a woman named Sally is not pretty, is she a blond?* and (2) *If Sally is not blond, is she pretty?* As Hersh et al. (1979) have pointed out, to the first question the concrete operational child typically reasons that *blond = pretty.* To the second question the concrete operational child typically reasons in terms of reciprocals and answers that Sally is *not* pretty. The comprehension of inverses is not evident in the child's reasoning.

For the non-formal operational child, the difficulty with this kind of problem is that it is *almost hypothetical* and requires knowledge about inverses of reciprocals. The problem is hypothetical in that the statement "all blonds are pretty" conflicts with the child's experience (i.e., all blonds are not pretty). Also, the inverse categories "not blond" and "not pretty" are *abstract* categories. For the child it is more difficult to concretely conceptualize inverse categories than it is to conceptualize the original categories or their reciprocals (Hersh et al., 1979).

Proportion

The development of children's concepts of proportion can be viewed in their actions with a seesaw balance of the type in Figure 9.[2] Before the age of 7, children have difficulty equalizing weights on a balance. They are aware that a balance is possible, but their attempts to attain it are always successive trial-and-error corrections. Compensation on the balance is never systematic. After age 7 (concrete operations) children discover a small weight can balance a larger weight by placing it farther from the fulcrum than

[2] The discussion of proportion is based on Piaget and Inhelder's book, *The Growth of Logical Thinking from Childhood to Adolescence*, 1958, pp. 164-181.

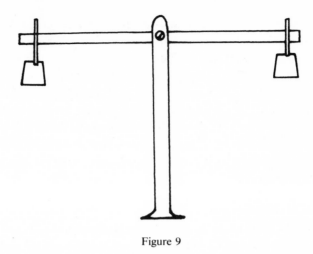

Figure 9

the larger weight. They learn to equalize weight and length in a systematic manner. But they do not coordinate the two functions of weight and length as a proportion.

Around age 13 comprehension of the proportion principle ($W/L = 2W/2L$) occurs when the child becomes aware that an increase in weight on one side of the fulcrum can be compensated for by an increase in distance from the fulcrum on the other side. Thus the development of the child's conception of proportion is consistent with his general conceptual development in that qualitative differences in schemata of proportion are found at different periods.

Conservation of Movement; the Pendulum Problem

A pendulum can be made to swing faster or slower by adjusting the length of the string holding it (the shorter the string the faster the movement). When asked to adjust the speed of a pendulum, concrete operational children typically insist on adjusting the weight of the pendulum. If they adjust the length of the string, they usually adjust the weight of the pendulum at the same time. They insist on attributing any change in the speed of the pendulum to the adjustment in the weight. Concrete operational children have difficulty separating the variables of weight and length.

During the period of formal operations, children learn to separate weight and length in the pendulum problem. By age 15, subjects are usually aware that the length of the string is the important variable affecting the speed of the pendulum (Inhelder and Piaget, 1958, pp. 67-79).

SUMMARY OF THE PERIOD OF FORMAL OPERATIONS

The period of formal operations is the culmination of the development of cognitive structures. Schemata typically reach maximum *qualitative* development by about age 16 or older; some adults never fully develop formal reasoning. The adolescent is able to think logically in relation to all classes of problems. He can solve hypothetical problems, verbal problems, and he can use scientific reasoning. The child with formal operations can think about his own thoughts and feelings. Formal operations evolve out of concrete operations. The processes of assimilation and accommodation constantly modify cognitive structures through the period of formal operations. Each structural change incorporates and improves upon previous structures. The process of development of schemata begins at birth and culminates in adolescence.

Chapter Seven

Cognitive Development
and Adolescence[1]

Adolescent behavior has always been a matter of concern
to parents, educators, and psychologists. Many theorists
have tried to account for the unique characteristics of the
adolescent period. Psychoanalytic theory (Freud, 1946;
Erickson, 1959) offers a rationalization for affective and
social aspects of adolescent behavior, though there has
been little supporting research for this position. Be-
haviorists by and large have avoided the topic of adolescence. While adolescence has received considerable attention in educational and psychological literature, little of
this attention has been concerned with the intellectual development of the older child and the possible effects of the
unique characteristics of adolescent reasoning on adolescent behavior.

One characteristic of adolescents is their ability to
"catch" adults by using illogical reasoning. Every teacher
and parent has experienced this persistent and sometimes
frustrating characteristic, which is not found in younger
children. It occurs in children with formal operations be-

---

[1] For present purposes, adolescence will be thought of as roughly
from 15 to 18 years. The adolescent is assumed to have developed
formal operations.

cause they have reasoning and logical abilities that are in some ways *equal* to those of adults. Like adults with formal reasoning, adolescents do not always use it, but once the reasoning is developed, adolescents have the same capabilities for reasoning as adults.

A major difference between adult and adolescent reasoning capabilities is the sheer *number of schemata*, or structures. The development of new schemata or new areas of knowledge does not stop with the attainment of formal operations. As people continue to have new experiences, they continue to develop new schemata and concepts. The adult's range of experiences typically has been much greater than the adolescent's. Thus, the typical adult possesses more structures or "content" to which he can apply his reasoning powers than does the typical adolescent.

The aspect of Piaget's work that has probably been most neglected is that which attempts to account for the uniqueness of adolescent thought and behavior. While Piaget does not attempt to explain all adolescent behavior, he does provide an important link between cognitive development and general behavior. It is unfortunate (in the opinion of the writer) that Piaget's thoughts on this topic have not attracted more interest and attention, particularly among parents and teachers of adolescents.

Piaget's explanation of adolescent behavior is consistent with the rest of his theory. He sees the unique characteristics of adolescent thought and personality as a normal outgrowth of development. That is, much of adolescent thought and behavior can be explained by prior development. In this respect the development of cognitive structures before and during adolescence helps to account for the characteristics of behavior during the age period.

The adolescent is typically one who has entered the period of formal operations and is developing, or has developed, the cognitive skills of that period. Logical operations permit the child to solve a wide range of logical problems. At this point the qualitative development of cognitive structures is presumed complete. The typical adolescent has the mental apparatus required to solve problems logically as well as adults can. Why then does the adolescent "think differently" from the adult?

Piaget believes the characteristics of adolescent thought that make him unique are in large measure due to the child's level of cognitive development and his accompanying *egocentrism* of thought during adolescence.

EGOCENTRISM AND ADOLESCENCE

Egocentrism is the constant companion of cognitive development. At each new stage of mental growth, the child's inability to differentiate assumes a unique form and is expressed in a novel set of behaviors. Thus, one of the characteristics of thought associated with *all* newly acquired cognitive structures is egocentrism. This can be thought of as a negative byproduct of mental development which, in a sense, distorts the initial use of newly acquired cognitive structures. Each period of development finds egocentrism manifest in a unique form.

During the sensori-motor period (0-2 years) the child is egocentric in the sense that he cannot differentiate between other objects and himself as an object, nor between objects and his sensory impressions. He is the center of his world. With development during the period, this type of egocentrism subsides. It disappears by the time the child becomes able to internally represent objects and events. The egocentrism of the preoperational period (2 to 7 years) is seen in the inability of children to differentiate between their own thoughts and those of others. The child believes his thoughts are always correct. The egocentrism of the preoperational period subsides as social interaction with others (particularly peers) increases. Elkind (1967) suggests the preoperational child is also egocentric in being unable to differentiate between symbols (words) and their referrents. The child of this period is seen to give incomplete verbal descriptions to others, believing that words carry more information than they really do (p. 1025).

During concrete operations (7 to 11 years) the child becomes able to apply logical operations to concrete problems. Egocentrism takes the form of inability to differentiate between perceptual events and mental constructions. The child cannot "think" independently of his perceptions. Hypotheses requiring perceptually untrue assumptions (coal is white) cannot be pursued. Only the attainment of formal operations permits this form of egocentrism to diminish.

As each new plane of cognitive functioning is initially characterized by a type of egocentrism, so too is adolescence. The adolescent, in a sense, becomes possessed with his new-found powers of logical thought. In adolescent thought, the criterion for making judgments becomes what is logical to the adolescent, not always what is realistic. The egocentrism of adolescence is the inability of the child to differentiate between his idealistic thought and the "real" world, The adolescent is emboldened with the egocentric belief in the omnipotence of logical thought. He can think logically about the future and about hypothetical people and events. He feels that the world should submit itself to idealistic (logical) schemes rather than to systems of reality. He does not understand that the world is not always rationally ordered, as he thinks it should be. Inhelder and Piaget (1958) write:

> . . . when the cognitive field is again enlarged by the structuring
> of formal thought, a . . . form of egocentrism comes into view.
> This egocentrism is one of the most enduring features of ado-

lescence ... the adolescent not only tries to adapt his ego to the social environment but, just as emphatically, tries to adjust the environment to his ego ... The result is a relative failure to distinguish between his point of view ... and the point of view of the group which he hopes to reform ... But we believe that, in the egocentrism found in the adolescent, there is more than a simple desire to deviate; rather, it is a manifestation of the phenomenon of lack of differentiation ... the adolescent goes through a phase in which he attributes an unlimited power to his own thoughts so that the dreams of a glorious future of transforming the world through ideas ... seems to be not only fantasy but also an effective action which in itself modifies the empirical world [pp. 343-346].

According to Piaget's formulation, to some extent the differences between the thought of adolescents and adults is in part a function of the normal course of cognitive development. Inhelder and Piaget (Ibid.) say:

We have seen that the principal intellectual characteristics of adolescence stem directly or indirectly from the development of formal structures. Thus, the latter is the most important event in the thinking found in this period [p. 347].

The adolescent becomes involved in an idealistic crisis. He has the powers of propositional logic, but he cannot distinguish between the new powers and society applying it to theories. It might seem that adolescents are doomed forever to be idealistic social critics. But, as the egocentrism of other periods gradually diminishes, so does the egocentrism of adolescence. Egocentrism subsides when the adolescent learns to use his logic effectively in relation to the reality of life, and not only in relation to life as he thinks it should be. Inhelder and Piaget (Ibid.) write:

... the focal point of the decentering process is the entrance into the occupational world or the beginning of serious professional training. The adolescent becomes an adult when he undertakes a real job. It is then that he is transformed from an idealistic reformer into an achiever. In other words, the job leads thinking away from the dangers of formalism back into reality [p. 346].

The *idealism* frequently apparent in adolescent reasoning can be viewed as "false" or incomplete idealism. What looks like idealism may in reality be reasoning based on an *egocentric* use of formal thought. When the typical adolescent makes judgments based on reasoning, his conclusions seem to be idealistic. But his logic and reasoning frequently do not take into account realities of human behavior that have nothing to do with logic.

Society confirms the biblical dictate "Thou shalt not kill," yet historically societies have sanctioned wars, the death penalty for certain crimes, and other "killings." Viewed from an adolescent's egocentric-logical point of view, these behaviors are illogical and thus wrong. The adolescent does not take into account the many *real* causes of human and societal behaviors that have nothing to do with logic. Similarly, parents instruct their children not to smoke or drink alcohol, although the parents engage in those activities. To the adolescent this seems illogical.

The adolescent must learn to assume adult (realistic) roles in the real world. This involves not only cognitive development but also a parallel affective development. The dilemma of human behavior is more than a logical problem, and it is this perspective that adolescents typically do not appreciate until they have encountered reality in a *serious* way. When the world is encountered as it really is, and not merely in a logical context, adaptations are made that permit a shift from a logical-egocentric perspective to a logical-realistic perspective. The capability for a realistic form of idealism occurs, an idealism able to appreciate the logical *and* non-logical complexities of problems.

American society has greatly extended the time adolescents and young adults spend at the stage of *false idealism*. Many people do not begin a "real job" until after college or even later. For them, the adaptation of logical reasoning to reality is clearly postponed.

The mental developments of adolescence are essential to the subsequent development of adult thought, but they do not ensure realistic adult thought. The implementation of formal thought in adolescence is initially egocentric. The adolescent does not differentiate between the many possible perspectives. Objectivity of thought with respect to conflicting issues is attained (and egocentrism lost) when the adolescent assumes adult roles in the real world and can differentiate the many possible points of view (Ibid., p. 345).

Chapter Eight

Summary of Intellectual Growth and Its Implications for Education

What has been presented so far is an introduction to Piaget's theory of cognitive development as it relates to intellectual growth. (Chapter Nine will present Piaget's theory on the development of the child's moral reasoning.) The basic elements of his work have been presented, though they have not been examined in detail. A realistic evaluation of Piaget's theory cannot be made if it is based only on the material presented in this book.

The attempt has been made to trace the logical development of the structures of intelligence from birth through adulthood. Hopefully the relationship between early sensori-motor development and later development has been established. Piaget's theory clearly suggests that the path of cognitive development is the same for all people. From his theory, a descriptive outline of cognitive development has emerged.

SUMMARY

During the sensori-motor period (0-2 years) the infant's reflexive behaviors gradually evolve into clearly intelligent behavior. Through maturation and active interaction with the environment (assimilation and accommodation), sensori-motor behaviors become increasingly differentiated and progressively evolve into intentional behaviors. The infant develops means-end problem-solving behavior. Before the age of 2, the child is able to mentally represent objects and events, and mentally (through representation) arrive at solutions to sensori-motor problems. The schemata of the 2-year-old are qualitatively and quantitatively superior to those of the younger child.

During the preoperational period (2 to 7 years) intellectual behavior moves from the sensori-motor level to the conceptual level. There is rapid spoken language development that accompanies the rapid conceptual development of the period. The development of spoken language is *not* seen as necessary for the development of reasoning to proceed. During the period the child's thought is egocentric, the child being unable to assume the viewpoints of others and believing everything he thinks is "right." In conservation problems he is unaware of transformations of states and tends to "center" on perceptual aspects of problems. Thought by age 7 is pre-logical. Conflicts between perception and reasoning are generally resolved in favor of perception.

The concrete operational child (7 to 11 years) develops the use of logical thought. By the end of the period he can solve the conservation problems and most "concrete" problems. During these years the logical operations of reversibility, seriation, and classification are developed. The child can think logically, but he cannot apply his logic to verbal, hypothetical, and abstract problems.

During the period of formal operations (11 to 15 years) cognitive structures (schemata) become qualitatively "mature." The child becomes structurally able to apply logical operations to all classes of problems. He can apply his logical thought to complex verbal problems, hypothetical problems, and problems involving the future. The child with formal operations can operate on an argument independent of its content. Logic becomes firmly available to

TABLE 2

Summary of the Periods of Cognitive Development

Period	Characteristics of the Period	Major Change of the Period
Sensori-motor (0-2 years)		Development proceeds from reflex acitvity to representation and sensori-motor solutions to problems
Stage 1 (0-1 months)	Reflex activity only No differentiation	
Stage 2 (1-4 months)	Hand-mouth coordination Differentiation via sucking reflex	
Stage 3 (4-8 months)	Hand-eye coordination Repeats unusual events	
Stage 4 (8-12 months)	Coordination of two schemata Object permanence attained	
Stage 5 (12-18 months)	New means through experimentation—follows sequential displacements	
Stage 6 (18-24 months)	Internal representation New means through mental combinations	

Preoperational (2-7 years)	Problems solved through representation—language development (2-4 years) Thought and language both egocentric Cannot solve conservation problems	Development proceeds from sensori-motor representation to pre-logical thought and solutions to problems
Concrete Operational (7-11 years)	Reversability attained Can solve conservation problems—logical operations developed and applied to concrete problems Cannot solve complex verbal problems and hypothetical problems	Development proceeds from pre-logical thought to logical solutions to concrete problems
Formal operations (11-15 years)	Logically solves all types of problems—thinks scientifically Solves complex verbal and hypothetical problems Cognitive structures mature	Development proceeds from logical solutions to concrete problems to logical solutions to all classes of problems

the child as a tool of thought. During adolescence, formal thought is egocentric. The adolescent tries to reduce all reasoning behavior to what is logical and has difficulty co-ordinating his ideals with what is real.

At each new level of cognitive development, previous levels are incorporated and integrated. The preoperational child does not throw away his sensori-motor schemata and take up new ones. Sensori-motor schemata are modified and improved. The processes of assimilation and accommodation permit the continuous development of cognitive structures. Schemata are continually being modified throughout life, from birth throughout adulthood. While qualitative changes in capabilities for logical reasoning cease after the development of formal operations, qualitative changes in content and function of intelligence continue. That is, people continue to develop concepts and purposes to which their reasoning can be applied.

Thus, early sensori-motor development is the foundation upon which later conceptual development is built. The basic paradigm of cognitive development for Piaget is seen as the assimilation and accommodation of experience, resulting in qualitative structural changes in cognitive machinery (schemata). In this sense, the child is truly father of the man.

Characteristics of Cognitive-Development Stages

Piaget's theory has been outlined as four major periods or stages across the continuum of development. Each period has been further divided into smaller substages. Every major change in development is one more step on the way to formal reasoning. Each step represents a qualitative change in reasoning abilities. The major stages share certain characteristics:

1. Each stage is characterized by qualitatively different reasoning. The reasoning of successive stages is always superior to the reasoning of previous stages.

2. Each stage or improvement in reasoning permeates the child's reasoning rather than affecting reasoning about a particular event. For example, the child who constructs a concept that the length of objects does not change when the position of the object changes (conservation of length) can use this new reasoning in situations where object length is relevant. Objects and space literally take on a new dimension for the child. Many structures are affected, not just one isolated structure.

3. At each new stage the child integrates the knowledge and reasoning of the previous stage into his "new" knowledge. Structures or schemata are changed (through adaptation), but prior formulations are never destroyed or eliminated. What was previously known remains with some improvements in the quality of knowledge. Each new level of reasoning is a *transformation* of prior reasoning and as such is not totally *new* but is now improved.

4. The stages of development are invariant. Formal reasoning cannot develop before concrete operations are developed. Concrete operations develop *only* after preoperational reasoning develops. Development always progresses from a less differentiated and less sophisticated level of reasoning to a more differentiated and more sophisticated level of reasoning.

Intelligence and Adaptation

For Piaget cognitive development is the intellectual counterpart of biological adaptation to the environment. As we adapt biologically to our environment, so too do we adapt intellectually. Through assimilation and accommodation the external world is organized and given structure. Schemata are the products of the organization.

Adaptation begins at birth with the exercise of sensorimotor reflexes. Differentiations via reflexes (sucking) are the first adaptations that are of eventual importance in cognitive development. As the child develops, the adaptations he makes are increasingly less related to sensory and motor behaviors alone, and may be less clearly seen as adaptations to the untrained eye.

The concept of adaptation is a concept of motivation. Adaptations occur when there is a "need" or value to the individual accompanying them. Adaptations, including intellectual adaptations, are neither automatic nor inevitable. The minds of children will not develop until they see some intellectual value *to them*.

Variables in Cognitive Development

The critical variables in cognitive development are: maturation, experience, social interaction, and equilibration. Piaget uses these terms in a general, not specific, way. He avoids the fruitless nature-nurture argument, whether intelligence is inherited (maturation) or learned (experience) by maintaining that each of the above variables is necessary for cognitive development but that none alone is sufficient to assure its occurrence. According to Piaget, the interaction of all four sets the course of development.

Two of the variables, maturation and equilibration, are not subject to any type of external control. The other two variables, experience and social interaction, are in part determined by external events. Experiential and social situations can be structured so the child has opportunities to act upon things and interact with others. Piaget recognizes the potential effect of the "right" experience at the "right" time. While such structuring can be done, whether or not these experiences are assimilated and accommodated is still controlled by equilibration, an internal process.

There have been very few studies directed at validating Piagetian concepts of social interaction as a factor in cognitive development. The bulk of Piagetian studies have been concerned with experience as a variable. In these studies, social class, culture, and schooling have been found to be important variables. Several studies have found moderate correlations between social class and performance on Piaget-style tasks. A study by the author (Wadsworth, 1968) found social class to be related to performance on conservation tasks in kindergarten, but not to whether students learned to conserve during the study. The suggestion was that lower-class children attain conservation concepts at a slower rate than middle-class children, but that when levels of development are equated, there is no difference in acquisition.

The question of whether schooling can affect structural development is an important one. Few would argue that schooling does not affect cognitive *content* and *function*. Children acquire information (content) in school that they might not encounter otherwise (e.g., the study of history, science, and English grammar). Also, children generally develop skills in applying knowledge (function), such as acquiring computational skills in arithmetic. These may be acquired *with or without* comprehension, depending on the availability of relevant structures necessary for comprehension at the time of "learning" the instruction. Regarding structure, most studies conclude that children attain concrete operations about age 6 or 7 regardless of whether there has been formal schooling. A number of studies report the development of formal operations much more related to schooling. Mermelstein and Schulman (1967) found no difference between schooled and unschooled children in acquisition of conservation skills (concrete operations). Sigel and Mermelstein (1965) similarly found no difference on conservation tasks, but they did find a difference in favor of schooled children on class inclusion tasks (formal operations). Goodnow and Bethon (1966) found no difference on conservation tasks, but they found schooling was related to learning tasks requiring combinatorial reasoning. Thus, it would seem that schooling, as it is traditionally carried out, plays a more important role in helping children acquire content and functions to which they can apply reasoning and knowledge (structures) than it does in aiding the development of structures. Also, the importance of schooling in developing cognitive structures *may be* more important in later than earlier periods. This question requires much more research.

Knowledge and Reality: A Construction

The developing child's knowledge of the world (and reality) is not a copy of the "objective" world. Each individual over the course of his development constructs knowledge and reality (through assimilation and accommodation). Physical, logical-mathematical, and social-arbitrary knowledge are not acquired directly but are constructed by the individual child. Piaget (1967) writes:

> The clearest result of our research on the psychology of intelligence is that even the structures most necessary to the adult mind, such as the logico-mathematical structures, are not innate in the child; they are built up little by little . . . There are no innate structures: every structure presupposes a construction. All these constructions originate from prior structures and revert, in the final analysis, . . . to the biological problem [pp. 149-150].

Some may question whether knowledge is a construction; most children around the same age, and most adults, seem to have similar concepts. It is true that many people have similar concepts, but this does not make the notion of construction less viable. The world we live in is a physical world containing a diversity of objects. For most children, wherever they live, the necessary physical ingredients are present to enable them to construct physical and logical-mathematical knowledge. For example, most children encounter trees and other plants. They have active experiences with trees, and so structures of trees are constructed. Because there are certain physical similarities and differences among trees, children "discover" and construct similar schemata of trees. It is therefore reasonable to expect children who live in the same or a similar environment to construct similar schemata. On the other hand, children reared in different environments, where the raw materials for construction of similar concepts are not present, cannot be expected to develop similar structures. Eskimo children may never see a tree growing. If their only source of wood is driftwood found in the ocean, this may become the material from which concepts of trees are built. Thus an Eskimo child or adult may have a concept of wood and tree as being rootless, leafless, and so on.

Thus the development of cognitive structures and knowledge is an evolutionary process that takes place within every individual. The change is manifest in the individual's schemata which are constantly undergoing change. The process of assimilation ensures that schemata will not be copies of reality; accommodation ensures that constructions will have a measure of correspondence to the real world (Elkind, 1969, p. 329).

IMPLICATIONS OF PIAGET'S THEORY FOR EDUCATION

The remainder of this chapter deals with what the author feels are some of the clearer implications of Piaget's theory for educational practice. Piaget has not directed his research towards education and teaching, but his theory of how children acquire knowledge and develop intellectually clearly provides much that is relevant to education. Many psychologists and educators have been interpreting and applying Piagetian theory over the past ten years, and some general implications for education are relatively clear. Clearly he has said much that is relevant to education. The application of his theory to educational practice requires that it be translated into applied settings. Obviously this requires considerable familiarity with the theory, much more than has been presented here. The implications suggested here are more general than specific.

Invariance of Concept Acquisition: When to Teach

Piaget's work states that cognitive structures (schemata) are developed in an invariant sequence. That is, the course of cognitive development, marked by the development of structures, is the same for all children, although the ages at which they attain particular structures may vary with intelligence and the social environment (Piaget and Inhelder, 1969, p. 153). Invariance was most clearly described in this work in the discussions of sensori-motor intelligence (Chapter Four) and the attainment of conservation skills (Chapters Four and Five). Research on the invariance concept, while not conclusive, tends to support Piaget's belief that acquisition of concepts is hierarchical and integrative in nature.

A word of caution. Piaget does not say that the sequence of cognitive development he describes is the only sequence in which schemata can be acquired. Piaget has described cognitive development, not determined how it *must* proceed. He does not preclude other possible sequences, though any other sequence would have to meet criteria that successive structures incorporate previous structures in an integrative and hierarchical fashion.

Assuming that concept acquisition is invariant, at least in Western cultures, then it makes educational sense to use Piaget's model of invariance in determining when to teach what. Curriculum sequences should be designed with children's changing cognitive status in mind. If curriculums do not take into account children's levels of conceptual development, learning with comprehension is going to be inefficient. Children will not learn (develop schemata) if they do not have the prerequisite cognitive skills.

Readiness to learn is of particular concern to educators of elementary school children, though it should be of concern at all levels of education. According to Piagetian theory, a child is "ready" to develop a particular concept when, and only when, he has acquired the schemata that are necessary (prerequisites).

How Knowledge Is Acquired

Possibly the most important and most revolutionary implication of Piaget's theory is that children construct knowledge from their actions on the environment. Physical knowledge is constructed through actions on objects. Legitimate concepts of trees can only be acquired from, and elaborated by, children's "acting on" trees. Pictures of trees, stories about trees, and reading about trees cannot develop knowledge of trees in young children. Logical-mathematical knowledge is constructed from actions on objects when the most important component is the child's *action*, and not the particular object. Number, length, and area concepts cannot be built up from hearing about them or reading about them. The construction of social-arbitrary knowledge is dependent on the child's action on, and interaction with, other people. Again, this form of knowledge cannot be directly transmitted through words or other symbols; it must be constructed.

For educators, the basic implication is clear. If an objective of education is to enhance children's acquisition of knowledge, educational methods need to be consistent with how children acquire knowledge.

Individual Differences

Piaget has concerned himself primarily with the general psychological processes in cognitive development. He has not directly concerned himself with the topic of individual differences, though the fact that differences between individuals do exist is implicit in all his work. The major factor in cognitive development is the interaction of maturation, experience, social interactions, and equilibration. Clearly, different individuals can be expected to differ with respect to each of these variables.

Since development can be traced back to biological factors before birth, there can clearly be inherited biological differences affecting cognitive development. These can be manifest in different rates of *maturation* of relevant physiological structures.

Experience is a second variable in development. No two children have the same experiences. The history of experiences is different for every human being. Even identical twins raised in the same home cannot be assumed to have had the "same" experiences. Accordingly, differences in prior experiences can contribute to "individual differences" in cognitive development.

As children have different histories of general experiences, so do they have different histories of social experiences or *social interaction*. Because social interaction does not become an effective variable in cognitive development until after the egocentrism of the preoperational period comes to rest, the value of interactions prior to that time is as experience, not as social interaction. After age 6 or 7 interactions assume their "social" value. Clearly one's history of interactions, whether they are as experience or social, vary from person to person contributing to individual differences.

Equilibration is conceptualized as the regulator of the relationship between assimilation and accommodation. It can be thought of as a mode or style of regulation. A given event may be assimilated or accommodated differently by different persons. Many factors can contribute to this source of individual differences.

Children can be expected to differ in their histories of maturation, experience, social interaction, and equilibration, and they can differ in how these factors interact to govern cognitive development. A clear expectation is that wide individual differences in conceptual development can be expected even in children of the same age. Among a group of 100 randomly selected 7- and 8-year-olds (probably second-graders), we would find that most would be in transition from preoperational reasoning to concrete operational reasoning. A smaller group would probably still be clearly preoperational, and another similar group would be concrete operational. We would also find some students who were early preoperational in their reasoning, and a few who were advanced concrete operational. Thus, among children close together in chronological age, we would expect to find levels of development ranging from early preoperational through late concrete operational. The same range of developmental levels would be found at any chronological age. Individual differences are great. Children at the extremes are certainly far apart in terms of the thinking, reasoning, and comprehension they can bring to academic work and what they can be expected to learn and comprehend.

Methods of Assessing Conceptual Development

Methods and procedures for assessing levels of conceptual development of children with respect to Piagetian concepts are needed. The Piagetian tasks can be used for diagnostic purposes to make such an assessment. A relatively complete description of how to use Piagetian principles to assess either a child's developmental level or his level of knowledge development regarding a particular concept can be found in Wadsworth (1978). This book also contains complete descriptions of, and procedures for, administering 29 tasks derived from Piaget's work that are suitable for children of pre-school through high school age. A test of conceptual development (intelligence) has been under development at the University of Montreal by Adrien Pinard and Monique Laurendeau (1964) for ten years. The test is being derived from Piaget's theory and represents an approach to test construction that is new. Conventional intelligence tests, such as the Stanford-Binet and the Wechsler scales, have been constructed by selecting items that reliably discriminate between chronological age groups. While these instruments are useful, a test such as the one being devised by Pinard should add an important dimension to assessing logical reasoning and thinking, something most tests do not do adequately.

Gagné and Piaget: Similarities and Differences

Another method of viewing conceptual development, while derived from a different theoretical position than the one presented here, seems useful in the context of Piaget's theory and teacher requirements. Robert Gagné

(1962, 1965, 1977) is an American educational psychologist concerned with learning. He is a behaviorist and thus approaches the question of learning from a different theoretical position than Piaget. What they have in common is that they both conceptualize learning (concept acquisition) as taking place in a manner that is orderly, sequential, integrative, and hierarchical.

Gagné (1962, 1965) conceptualizes all learning as a function of prior learning, or prerequisite learnings. Learning of a particular concept only occurs if the concepts (or learnings) that are prerequisites to the concept have been acquired. Every bit of learning is thought of as generating a hierarchy in which prerequisite learnings can be identified (see Fig. 10). These prerequisites must be "learned" before the learning at the top of the hierarchy can occur. Gagné (1962) suggests hierarchies can be derived logically in certain content areas such as arithmetic and science. Hierarchies can be derived by beginning with a final learning task one is interested in and asking oneself the question: "What kind of capability would an individual have to possess if he were able to perform this task successfully, were we to give him only instructions?" (p. 356). Through systematic analysis, hierarchies of learnings can be derived in which lower members in the hierarchy serve as prerequisite learnings to higher members and all serve as prerequisites to the final learning. Experimental testing of such logically derived hierarchies have yielded predictable results (Gagné, 1962).

The similarity in Gagné's and Piaget's writings is that they both, in some respects, yield similar and useful ways for conceptualizing learning and for determining the level at which children can learn. They both see knowledge as accumulating in an orderly, sequential, and hierarchical manner. Both suggest there is an invariant order in which concepts may successfully be acquired.

Figure 10
Hypothetical Hierarchy of
Prerequisite Learning

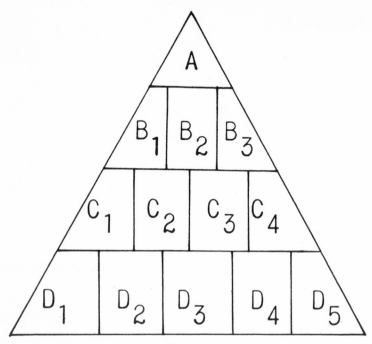

Since the writer has taken the liberty of suggesting that a behaviorist and developmentalist have something in common, it is important to indicate their main differences. Probably the most crucial point is with respect to the importance of "experience" in learning. According to Piaget, the organization of experience occurs within the organism (assimilation and accommodation) and the organism gives structure to experience. Thus, since organization is an internal process, external organization, such as the logical sequencing of learning experiences, cannot ensure internal organization. Gagné's position is that external organization is a necessary condition to optimize learning. The cognitive position assumes organization lies within the individual. The behaviorist position assumes organization is external to the individual.

Teaching Methods and Materials: How to Teach

Piaget's theory suggests that teaching methods and materials should be consistent with children's levels of conceptual development. *Active interactions* of the child with the environment (physical and social interactions) are seen as the most important school-related factor in cognitive development. Regarding school experiences and cognitive development, Piaget (1964) writes:

> Experience is always necessary for intellectual development ... but I fear that we may fall into the illusion that being submitted to an experience (a demonstration) is sufficient for a subject to disengage the structure involved. But more than this is required. The subject must be active, must transform things, and find the structure of his own actions on the objects [p. 4].

Cognitive reorganization resulting from assimilation and accommodation can only come about through the actions of the child. Thus actions, physical or cognitive, must occur if cognitive reorganization is going to take place. It must also be remembered that, according to Piaget, assimilation and accommodation of actions are always under internal control (equilibration) and reorganization of cognitive structures in a particular way can never be *ensured* by external organization of experience. A child's reorganization is always his own.

Through the period of concrete operations, manipulation of objects and materials dealing with concepts to be learned is most important. Seriation schemata (A < B, B < C thus A < C) can best be developed in concrete operational children if they visually and manually manipulate objects employing the concepts to be learned. In a similar manner, equivalence concepts (A = B, B = C, thus A = C) can best be learned if the child acts on objects that employ the concept. Reversibility in mathematical operations can be facilitated in children's learning if problems in multiplication and division are placed in opposition to one another (initially using concrete materials such as blocks) (14 × 3_____; 42 ÷ 3_____; 42 ÷ 14_____). The same principle holds true for reversibility learnings in simple addition and subtraction. Problems placed in opposition demonstrate reversibility and help facilitate accommodation to the concept (5 + 4_____; 9 - 4_____; 9 - 5_____). Through the concrete operational period, concrete experiences generate conceptual development.

With the attainment of formal operations, children become able to develop some logical-mathematical concepts without the aid of direct physical experience. At this level, the activity of the child can be purely representational and independent of any "concrete" experience. The child can act on verbally presented conceptual material. Conceptual development can proceed based on the child's actions on written and verbal materials. Of course, even the adolescent or adult with formal operations needs concrete experiences in order to develop *new* physical knowledge. If one has never had any experience with sailboats, it is difficult to acquire any useful knowledge about them.

Motivation: Spontaneous Interest and Surprise

Children are *motivated* to restructure their knowledge when they encounter experiences that conflict with their predictions. Piagets calls such an occurrence *disequilibration*, and the result, disequilibrium. Some have called it *cognitive conflict* or *conflict inducement*. To the extent that educators are interested in helping children acquire knowledge (as it is defined here) they must develop methods that encourage disequilibrium and permit children to carry out, in their own ways, the re-establishment of equilibrium through active methods (assimilation and accommodation). How can disequilibrium be recognized and encouraged by the teacher? Wadsworth (1978) suggests that children be permitted to explore many of their *spontaneous interests.* Such interests, frequently unique to the individual child, reflect disequilibrium and are sources of motivation. Teachers must find ways to permit children to follow their spontaneous interests. It is essential that teachers view such expenditures of time as valid from the point of view of intellectual development.

Another approach suggested by Wadsworth (1978) is for teachers to use *surprise* to elicit disequilibrium. Teachers cannot predict what will function as "surprise" to all students, but they can structure experiences to have outcomes that teachers expect are not predictable by most students.[1]

Social Interactions with Peers

Peer interactions become important with respect to cognitive development when the child becomes able to assimilate the viewpoints of others when they are different from his own. This comes about when the egocentrism of preoperational thought is dispelled around age 6 or 7. Accord-

[1] Further discussions of motivation viewed from a Piagetian perspective can be found in Wadsworth (1978) and Forman and Kuschner (1977).

ingly, peer interactions are of cognitive importance from the time the child enters school. Children learn to evaluate their egocentric thoughts by comparing them to the thoughts of others. About the age of 6 or 7 most children become able to accommodate to the views of others. Thus peer interactions can be a fruitful means of stimulating natural cognitive conflicts that can generate accommodation to the views of others and evaluation of one's own concepts. Social-arbitrary knowledge, a knowledge that is created by humans, is constructed by children from their interaction with others. Social-arbitrary knowledge cannot be acquired independently of other people (physical and logical-mathematical knowledge can). To the extent that educational programs purport to "teach" social knowledge, legitimate opportunities for interaction with others must be provided.

All types of situations in school that involve peer interactions are legitimate: role-playing, games, play, etc. They all stimulate peer interaction. Interactions can be centered on pertinent concepts. Conceptual development can be facilitated by making use of peer activities.

Sensori-Motor Development and Later Cognitive Development

Development resulting from motor and sensory behavior during the first two years of life is the bedrock upon which later cognitive development is built. The ability to represent objects as images and symbols develops from the reflex activities of the infant. Under "normal" conditions the child's actions in the environment ensure adequate development during the sensori-motor period and prepare the child for preoperational development. But this is not always the case. Development during the first two years of life can be impaired and affect later development.

The use of Piagetian concepts of sensori-motor develop-

ment as they pertain to education and learning are reflected best in the work of Newell Kephart. Kephart was a
clinician primarily interested in learning problems that
could be traced to faulty learning in early childhood and
how these problems could be corrected. Kephart evolved,
independently of Piaget, a diagnostic and remedial program for children with severe, non-physiological learning
problems that in practice closely parallels Piaget's theory
with respect to sensori-motor development. Kephart's
views are most comprehensively dealt with in his book,
The Slow Learner in the Classroom (1960, 1971), and are
outlined elsewhere (Kephart, 1964; Grzynkowicz and
Kephart, 1975). According to Kephart (Ibid.), the child's
first interactions with his environment are motor; his first
learnings and attempts to organize the environment are
based on these motor interactions. Learning difficulty can
begin during the motor stage if the child develops limited
motor *skills* instead of general motor *patterns*. A motor
skill is a specific motor act, such as walking, which is
limited in application. The motor skill of walking permits
the young child to place one foot in front of the other, but
it may not permit him to solve problems in walking, such
as getting around or over objects if it is an inflexible skill.
A motor pattern of walking is more generalized and useful
in solving motor problems. Only through the development
of flexible motor patterns does the child develop a stable
body of motor information about his environment.

With the development of a number of motor patterns,
such as locomotion, manipulation, balance, throwing and
catching, the child evolves a stable body of useful information about his environment. The initial information is
motor. Information processing is on a motor level. For
further progress, the child's system of motor knowledge
must be transferred to objects in his environment that he
cannot touch and manipulate. Since he cannot investigate

these objects in a motor fashion, he must learn to investigate perceptually. At this point though, perceptual data (obtained through vision and hearing) are not organized as motor data are organized. Perceptual data come to be organized by projecting motor organization onto perceptual data.

The transfer of the structure of motor data to perceptual data is called the "perceptual-motor match" by Kephart. Concepts useful to the child are initially motor. When motor patterns become stable, the child can begin to transfer the motor organization. As the child manipulates objects and receives motor data, he also watches the manipulation and receives unstructured visual data. Exploration with the eyes duplicates exploration with the hands. As the child repeatedly receives structured motor data and unstructured visual data, the visual data comes to take on the structure of the motor data through the perceptual-motor match. When the visual data become structured in the same way as the motor data (after the perceptual-motor match is complete) then, and only then, do visual data have enough structure to adequately evaluate events in the environment. Unlike motor evaluations, perceptual evaluations can be made of all objects and events that can be perceived. Distant objects can be construed as well as those close at hand.

According to Kephart, inadequacies in development can occur at several points. Children may fail to develop initial motor patterns from which useful perceptual patterns may be transferred. Second, the perceptual-motor match may not occur or may not be completed. If this happens, the child will have problems developing a stable and useful perceptual world. For example, suppose a child does not develop a motor pattern of the spatial relationships of "up," "down" and "right," "left." He cannot then transfer the motor relationship to perceptual data and may not develop stable perceptual awarenesses of the relationships. He may not be able to "see" the difference between up and down and right and left. This might not become evident until the child enters school and receives reading instruction. A child developing as described may be unable to "see" the difference between "b" and "p," or between "d" and "q," or between "M" and "W." These pairs of letters may look alike to the child and make learning how to read rather difficult.

According to Kephart's formulation, an inability to differentiate between letters (shapes) may be traced to faulty learning during motor development. The number of different problems of the type that have been described are innumerable. Both Piaget and Kephart agree that people "learn" to perceive (see and hear). Learning can be faulty or inefficient and may require correction. It is unfortunate that many of the symptoms of faulty early learning do not show up until the child is in second or third grade. Also, many children may be inappropriately labeled brain damaged, dyslexic, perceptually handicapped, or retarded (or a host of other names that all smack of organic impairment) when the real problem is a matter of motor or perceptual learning.

Under normal conditions the child's environment presents him with enough situations requiring him to make enough accommodations and adaptations to ensure adequate perceptual and motor development. When deficits do occur, specific remediation is required. Specific suggestions for dealing with specific perceptual-motor learning problems are provided by Kephart in *The Slow Learner in the Classroom* (1960, 1971), and in *Steps to Achievement for the Slow Learner* (1968), as well as a number of other of his works (Grzynkowicz and Kephart, 1975).

Educational Intervention and Piaget

There is great concern in educational circles as to whether educational intervention offers a solution to the problems of the "disadvantaged" and other deprived groups of children. Can conceptual development be speeded up? Can early intervention (preschool) compensate for social class differences in academic "readiness"? Piaget's theory of cognitive development does not provide a clear answer to these questions. Development is a function of the interaction of maturation, experience, social interaction, and equilibration. Presumably, within the limitations of maturation and equilibration, experiences (both social and general) can be manipulated. This does not ensure the child will act on the elements in a situation and assimilate and accommodate according to a formula. Piaget does not say how or under what specific conditions conceptual development can be advanced. In addition, the consequences of advancing development are not clear. Unfortunately for education, Piaget has been concerned with how concepts develop and not how to develop concepts.

Ten years ago, authorities on Piaget's work generally suggested that early intervention and efforts to help children acquire knowledge would not be fruitful. Elkind (1969) wrote:

> . . . the Piagetian conception of intelligence provides no support either for those who advocate formal preschool instruction or for those who argue for new methods and materials to stimulate intrinsic motivation [p. 335] .

Comments by Kohlberg (1968) were only slightly more encouraging:

> I have claimed that a Piagetian conception of methods of accelerating intellectual development (employing cognitive conflict, match, and sequential ordering of experience), a

Piagetian focus upon basic intellectual operations, and a Piagetian procedure of assessment of general intellectual development might generate somewhat more general and long-range cognitive effects than would other approaches.

Basically, however, the Piaget approach does not generate great optimism as to the possibility of preschool acceleration of cognitive development (or of compensation for its retardation) nor does it lead to a rationale in which such acceleration (or compensation) is especially critical during the preschool years [p. 1056].

In the past 10 years this negative conclusion has been substantially eroded. Most Piagetians now believe that school experiences can have an impact on children's acquisition of knowledge *if* teaching practices are brought in line with children's ways of learning (Wadsworth, 1978). Kagan (1976) provides evidence that some functional retardation is even reversible. Most Piagetians agree that teachers can help facilitate cognitive development, but most argue for an "enrichment" approach that permits children to solidify and generalize the knowledge they have, rather than for an acceleration approach. The long-term effects of acceleration are still not clear.

A WORD ABOUT TEACHING

As an educational psychologist, the writer feels one of the most important determinants of teachers' behaviors with respect to students is how they (the teachers) conceptualize phenomena. The classic example can be seen in the nature-nurture controversy that has pervaded psychology for years. If a teacher conceptualizes intelligence (the ability to succeed in school) as "fixed," she (or he) is probably not going to be motivated to try very hard to help a student who is a poor performer in the classroom. On the other hand, a teacher who conceptualizes intelligence as "developed," not fixed, may be motivated to help the poor performer. How teachers conceptualize intelligence and learning will influence their actions. Teachers' expectations of how children can perform in the classroom are derived from their conceptualizations. The fact that teacher expectations (as well as parental expectation and self-expectation) are communicated to students and affect their achievement has been well documented (Rosenthal and Jacobsen, 1968). How teachers conceptualize will have a lot to do with how much is learned, and who learns, in their classrooms.

The writer believes Piaget's conceptualizations (theory) are a set that are at once comprehensive and useful. They offer an alternative way of conceptualizing behavior and development for those interested in psychology and education. At best, psychology as a science operates on the level of theories. There are no laws in psychology (as in physics or chemistry), so one must be content with using theories and try to find those that are most useful. All theories in psychology are constantly changing, being validated, tested, and reorganized. To ask if a theory is "right" or "wrong" is a poor question. Some theories are useful for explaining one phenomenon and useless for explaining another. Thus the user of theories (and conceptualizations) must pick and choose with care. Generally, acceptance or rejection of a theory is a function of its utility in predicting behavior, its persuasive power, its logic, and its novelty. All these criteria continue to reflect the appeal of Piaget's work.

There is little doubt that Piaget's theory of cognitive development will continue to change and become more refined, as it has over the years. Some of his concepts may not stand up in the face of future research. Others certainly will. The writer has presented a look at the part of

Piaget's conceptualizations that seem to be most important for education. Needless to say, the implications of Piaget's concepts for education have not been exhausted in this work. The author's interpretations of Piaget's writings have produced some implications that are very general in nature. They are not remedies for educational problems. They are a start. Piaget's work over the last fifty years has generated a degree of interest and inquiry that is unprecedented and shall continue for many years. The writer hopes an interest in Piaget's concepts has been generated here.

Chapter Nine

New Development of
Moral Reasoning in the Child

A popular and valid interest in education today is the development of moral and social reasoning. This includes such concepts as values, ethics, and, to some extent, the development of emotion and affect. Recent years have witnessed the rise of the values-clarification movement in education, as well as considerable research and writing about *moral development*. In addition, there has always been some expression of concern that people like Piaget seem to have directed their attention almost entirely to intellectual growth and little to emotional, affective, and social development.

Certainly Piaget has focused his efforts on the development of knowledge. Most of his research and writings deals with *physical* and *logical-mathematical* knowledge. Nevertheless, Piaget has not neglected the development of *social-arbitrary* knowledge in children. The study of values, ethics, observation of social rules, and emotion and affect is part of the development of what Piagetians call social-arbitrary knowledge. Piaget's *The Moral Judgment of the Child* (1965), originally published in 1932, is his major work on the development of social and moral concepts in children. In *The Moral Judgment of the Child*

152

Piaget outlined his investigation of children's development of concepts of rules and rule-following behavior, clumsiness and accidents, stealing, lying, and justice. In this early work Piaget showed that children's social concepts are constructed, and that their construction of moral concepts closely parallels their distinction of intellectual concepts in general. Piaget returned briefly to the topic of moral reasoning in *The Psychology of the Child* (Piaget and Inhelder, 1969). His views remained unchanged over the years. *The Psychology of the Child* is, in part, a restatement and clarification of the earlier work.

The publication of *The Moral Judgment of the Child* in 1932 presented a conception of the child, and of moral reasoning, that was radical at the time, which may explain why this work seems to have been overlooked for many years. Hersh, Paolitto, and Reimer (1979) suggest that the field of psychology was not ready in the 1930s for Piaget's research and writing on moral judgment. Piaget's conclusion that thought(s) and feelings developed in a parallel fashion and that one level of cognitive development placed constraints on feelings and moral judgment was a foreign idea to a psychology immersed in the Freudian concept that reasoning and feeling were separate and that morality sprang primarily from events in early life. Not until the late 1950s was Piaget's work on moral judgment "discovered" by a small segment of American psychologists. At that time Lawrence Kohlberg (1958, 1969, 1976) began research at Harvard University into children's moral judgments. Kohlberg's work has built primarily on Piaget's *The Moral Judgment of the Child*. More recent work by Robert Selman (1971) on role taking and by William Damon (1975) on positive justice also grew in part out of Piaget's work. Psychologists like Henry Dupont (in press) have recently been looking at Piaget's work and its relationship to the development of affect (feelings, emotions, etc).

The late 1960s and the 1970s have seen an increased interest in aspects of development that are not purely cognitive. Piaget dealt with these issues early in his career, and much of the research being done today arose out of Piaget's work. Piaget's book on moral judgment remains an exciting and "fresh" piece of work; the research done in recent years has not made Piaget's work outdated. The major conclusions of his book, revolutionary in 1932, remain intact.

CHILDREN'S CONCEPTS OF RULES

To investigate children's understanding of rules, Piaget (1965)[1] asked children questions about the rules of a child's game. The game was marbles, requiring two or more players. Marbles was viewed by Piaget as an appropriate activity for study because it was a social game with a structure of rules. These rules may vary from place to place, but there are always rules. Marbles was, and is, a popular game among children in Geneva.

Piaget interviewed twenty boys and girls, 4 to 13 years in age, regarding their understanding of the rules. The questions that Piaget directed to the children were designed to determine whether the rules of the game were externally determined, just, and alterable. Thus, such questions as "What are the rules [of marbles]?" "Show me how to play," "Can you invent a new rule?" and "Is it a fair rule?" are typical. In these interviews with children the experimenter functions both as a participant and an observer. The experimenter actually plays the game with the chil-

---

[1] The reference for the remainder of this chapter is Piaget (1965) unless otherwise noted.

dren in order to learn the child's way of playing (Gruber and Voheche, 1977, pp. 156-157). Piaget writes:

> The experimenter speaks more or less as follows. "Here are some marbles. . . . You must show me how to play. When I was little I used to play a lot, but now I've quite forgotten how to. I'd like to play again. Let's play together. You'll teach me the rules and I'll play with you." . . . You must avoid making any sort of suggestions. All you need do is to appear completely ignorant [about the game of marbles] and even make intentional mistakes so that the child may each time point out clearly what the rule is. Naturally, you must take the whole thing very seriously, all through the game. Then you ask who has won, and why, and if everything is not quite clear, you begin a new set [p. 24].

In addition to questions about the rules, Piaget asked children to give the reasoning behind their answers. As we have seen, it is children's reasoning rather than their answers per se that usually provides the most information about their knowledge and concepts.

Piaget found that there were four broad stages in the development of children's knowledge of the rules of marbles. These stages clearly parallel Piaget's four stages of cognitive development. Piaget's stages will be summarized here as the (1) motor stage, (2) egocentric stage, (3) stage of cooperation, and (4) stage of codification of rules.

Stage 1: Motor Stage

In Piaget's first stage of comprehension of rules, the motor stage, the child does not seem to be aware of any rules or that rules are obligatory. During the first few years of life, frequently extending into the preoperational period of cognitive development, marbles are played with according to habit and in any way the child wants. There is no "game," and so there are no rules. At this stage, children play with marbles by themselves. The activity is non-social. Marbles are primarily objects to be explored (physical knowledge). The child's enjoyment seems to come largely from the motoric or muscular manipulation of the marbles. There is no evidence of any awareness of a game in the social sense.

Stage 2: Egocentric Stage

Usually between the ages of 2 and 5, children become aware of the existence of rules and begin to want to "play the game" with other, usually older, children. Young children begin by imitating older children's play, but the cognitively egocentric child continues to play *by himself*, without trying to "win." In the same way, children's early preoperational use of spoken language is characterized by asocial collective monologues (egocentric); their play in groups is characterized by a lack of any social interaction or true cooperation. Piaget's observation helps illustrate the point.

> Loeff (6) often pretends to by playing with Mae [another boy] . . . he immediately begins to "fire" at the marbles assembled in a heap and plays without either stopping or paying any attention to us. "Have you won?—*I don't know, I think I have.—Why?—Yes, because I threw the mibs* [marbles] —and I?—*Yes, because you threw the mibs*" [p. 38].

At this stage of reasoning about rules, children believe everyone can win. Rules are viewed as fixed, and respect for them is unilateral.

What seems to be asocial behavior, egocentrism, and isolated play is actually an advance over the behavior of the previous stage from a social point of view. The child wants to play with other children and attempts to adapt socially by imitating other children. Still, the egocentric child typically lacks any appreciation or knowledge of the game from a social point of view. He imitates what he sees, but does not yet reason like his older playmates. Thus his "play" does not involve cooperation. But because adaptations are attempted, the child's behavior represents an advance over the behavior of the earlier stage.

Stage 3: Stage of Cooperation

Usually around 7 or 8 years of age (the beginning of the concrete operational period of reasoning), children begin to grasp the significance of rules for proper game playing. Cooperation in a social sense begins to emerge. Rules are no longer seen as absolute and unchangeable. Children typically develop the notion that the rules of the game can be changed if all agree to the change. Children begin to try to *win* (a social act) while conforming to the rules of the game. Piaget writes:

> In seeking to win the child is trying above all to contend with his partners *while observing common rules.* The specific pleasure of the game ceases to be muscular [Stage 1] and egocentric [Stage 2] and becomes social [p. 42].

For the child who is beginning to demonstrate cooperation, the aim of the game is no longer to knock the marbles out of the circle or square but to *win* (in a competitive sense).

While cooperation is evident in Stage 3 children, they typically do not know the rules of the game in detail, and many discrepancies are apparent between children's reports of what the rules are. This lack of agreement about the rules and the emphasis on winning can be observed in practically any group of young children engaged in a game.

If permitted, they will spend more time arguing about what the rules are, in an effort to win, than they actually spend playing the game.

Stage 4: Codification of Rules

Around the beginning of formal operations, about age 11 or 12, most children develop a relatively sophisticated understanding of rules. The rules of the game are seen as

fixed at any point in time by mutual agreement and changeable through mutual agreement. The earlier belief that rules are permanent and externally imposed by an authority is no longer present. At this stage, the rules in use are known to all, and all agree on what the rules are. Children recognize fully that rules are necessary for cooperation and to play the game effectively. There also seems to be an interest in rules for their own sake.

Piaget suggests that children's knowledge and comprehension of rules develop over a period of time in a manner that closely parallels their general intellectual growth. Children's earliest play is asocial, habitual, and reflects no understanding or awareness of rules. Advanced preoperational children generally are aware of rules, but their play is egocentric and not based on cooperation. Rules at this point are *coercive*, based on unilateral respect. By early adolescence, children usually begin to understand that game rules are outgrowths of cooperation and necessary for fair play.

Piaget reminds us that the stages of development with respect to rules are not entirely separate; they run together. Children's development proceeds along a continuum; dividing the continuum into stages is for our convenience and does not reflect real breaks in the developmental continuum.

> These stages must, of course, be taken only for what they are worth. It is convenient for the purposes of exposition to divide the children up into age-classes or stages, but the facts present themselves as a continuum which cannot be cut up into sections [p.17].

CONCEPTS OF ACCIDENTS AND CLUMSINESS

Parents and teachers of pre-school and early elementary children know that children frequently have difficulty viewing other children's accidents as "accidents." For example, one child may bump into another "accidentally." The child who has been bumped typically views the act as intentional and worthy of appropriate retribution. Endless classroom scuffles are initiated by such accidents or clumsiness. Young children are unable to appreciate other children's *intentions*, or to see another child's point of view, and parents are frustrated in their attempts to explain to young children that accidents and clumsiness on the part of others does not deserve punishment. The problem is that young children typically have not yet *constructed concepts of intentionality*. They firmly believe in the moral credo "an eye for an eye, and a tooth for a tooth," and in its application in all cases. Piaget's work suggests that until children construct the necessary moral reasoning capability, reasoning alone cannot dissuade them from retributive acts. They are simply not capable of understanding.

Piaget interviewed children to discover their concepts and beliefs about clumsiness and accidents. He used pairs of stories that contrasted children's intentions against the quantitative results of their "accidents." Children were asked to compare the accidents in the two stories to decide which was worse, and to explain their selection. One pair of stories Piaget used follows:

> A. A little boy who is called John is in his room. He is called to dinner. He goes into the dining room. But behind the door there was a chair, and on the chair was a tray with fifteen cups on it. John couldn't have known that there was all this behind the door. He goes in, the door knocks against the tray, bang go the fifteen cups and they all get broken!

> B. Once there was a little boy whose name was Henry. One day when his mother was out he tried to get some jam out of the cupboard. He climbed up on a chair and stretched out his arms. But the jam was too high up and he couldn't reach it and have any. But while he was trying to get it he knocked over a cup. The cup fell down and broke [p. 122].

Piaget found that among children younger than 7 or 8 years, the boy in the first story, John, is usually viewed as having committed a "worse" act. John's actions are typically viewed as worse than Henry's because John broke *15*

cups while Henry broke only *1 cup*. The children's judgments are based on the concrete or quantitative results of
the actions. John broke more cups, and that's that! There
is no appreciation yet of *intention* in judging actions.
Motives are not considered.

Around the age of 8 or 9 years, children typically *begin*
to be able to consider events from someone else's point of
view. This parallels a reduction in egocentric thought. Children begin to see that motives and intentions are *as important* as the results of actions. Piaget recorded the following
responses and reasoning of a 9-year-old to the above
stories.

> Corm (9): "*Well, the one who broke them as he was coming
> isn't naughty, 'cos he didn't know there was any cups. The
> other one wanted to take the jam and caught his arm on a cup
> —*Which one is naughtiest;—*The one who wanted to take the
> jam.—*How many cups did he break?—*One.—*And the other
> boy?—*Fifteen.—*Which one would you punish most?—*The boy
> who wanted to take the jam. He knew, he did it on purpose"*
> [p. 129].

Increasingly, intentions become more important than the
consequences of a particular action. This comes about only
when children are able to view actions from the point of
view of others (pp. 132-137). Children's ability to understand and consider intentions begins to develop when egocentrism of thought diminishes. Children progress from a
less social to a more social form of cooperative reasoning,
similar in nature to their comprehension-understanding of
rules.

Unfortunately, Piaget's views do not offer any hope that
young children can be "taught" to understand other children's "accidents." Children under 7 years of age generally
do not have a concept of intentions and are thus incapable
of understanding the "accidents" of others. The under-

standing of intentions cannot be "taught" to young children through verbal methods. According to Piaget, each child must *construct* the concept out of his or her active interactions with others. Peers are particularly important in this process. Until a child constructs a concept of intentionality and becomes capable of taking the viewpoint of others, he or she will not understand reasoning that involves intentions and motives. Piaget's findings help us to understand young children's responses to the accidents and clumsiness of others, but do not solve the problem of what to do about such behavior.[2]

---

[2] The obvious implication in this situation is to realize all children cannot understand intentions and consequently cannot respond to reasoning. This does not mean you have to excuse the child who hits another child who accidently bumped into him. On the contrary, it means you cannot expect the child to *understand* an argument that involves intentions. The only solution is to forbid children to hit other children, and punish them when they do and reward them when they do not. On the other hand, some *accidents* and their *retributions* may be necessary for children to be prompted to construct the concepts involved. Young children typically understand that they themselves have *accidents* before they appreciate the accidents of others. Certainly the ability to take the view of another requires interactions with others.

CHILDREN AND LYING

Another interesting social and moral topic Piaget investigated is the development of children's concepts about lying. Parents and teachers frequently observe a great deal of what they would call lying among young children. Understandably, this can be a source of great concern to adults. Many parents ask themselves if they are rearing a "liar." What Piaget learned about children's concepts of lying may help us understand these behaviors. In his research Piaget asked children questions to determine their definition of a lie, and why one should not lie.

What Is a Lie?

Before the age of 6 or 7 years, most children view a lie as something that is "naughty." In addition, young children usually consider involuntary errors to be lies.

> Nus (6): "What is a lie?—*It's when you say naughty words.*— Do you know any naughty words?—*Yes.*—Tell me one.— *Charogne* [Corpse]. Is it a lie?—*Yes.*—Why?—*Because you mustn't say naughty words.*—When I say 'Fool!' is it a lie?— *Yes.*" . . .
>
> Rad (6): "*A lie is words you musn't say, naughty words*" [p. 143].
>
> Web (6): Once there was a boy who didn't know where the Rue des Acacias was [the street where Web lives]. A gentleman asked him where it was. The boy answered 'I think it's over there, but I'm not sure.' And it wasn't over there! Did he make a mistake, or did he tell a lie?—*It was a lie.*—Did he make a mistake or not make a mistake?—*He made a mistake.*—Then it wasn't a lie?—*He made a mistake and it was a lie*" [pp. 143-144].

Between the age of 6 or 7 and age 10 or so, a lie is typically viewed as something that is *not true*. A false statement is viewed as a lie regardless of the intent. If it is not true, it is a lie.

Chap (7): "What is a lie?—*What isn't true, what they say that they haven't done.*—Guess how old I am.—*Twenty.*—No, I'm thirty. Was it a lie what you told me?—*I didn't do it on purpose.*—I know. But is it a lie all the same, or not?—*Yes, it is all the same, because I didn't say how old you really were.*—Is it a lie?—*Yes, because I didn't speak the truth.*—Ought you to be punished?—*No.*—Was it naughty or not naughty?—*Not so naughty.*—Why?—*Because I spoke the truth afterwards!*" [p. 144].

It is as if children define a lie as a moral fault. Only after the age of 10 or 11 do children begin to recognize intentions in relation to lying. At this level of reasoning a lie is defined as something that is *intentionally false*. As we have seen with the previous moral concepts, an appreciation of intentions is not attained in most children until the development of formal operations.

Why One Should Not Lie

Piaget reports that when questioned about why one should not lie, the reason typically given children through age 7 years or so is, "You get punished." A typical child's report follows:

Zamb (6): "Why must we not tell lies?—*Because God punishes them.*—And if God didn't punish them?—*Then we could tell them*" [p. 168].

Punishment is the criterion used to determine whether a lie is permissible or not. According to young children, one does not tell a lie because of the punishment it can bring. But if there is no punishment, it is perfectly acceptable to tell lies.

For the older child, after age 9 or so, there is a separation of the concept of lie from punishment. At this point in development children typically believe that a lie is wrong even if it goes unpunished. Piaget observed:

> Gir (9): "Why is it naughty [a lie]?—*Because we get pun-ished.*—If you didn't know you had told a lie, would it be naughty too?—*It would be naughty, but less naughty....* Why would it be naughty?—*Because it is a lie all the same*" [p. 169].

Here, the rule is viewed by the child as obligatory and independent of punishment. There is clearly an element of cooperation in the child's reasoning, although rules are still seen as imposed by authorities on children rather than as an integral part of cooperation.

Piaget observed that a maturing of children's concepts about lying generally occurs around the age of 10 to 12. Intentions become the major criteria used to evaluate lying. The older child also recognizes that *not lying* is necessary for social cooperation. Children come to oppose lying because "truthfulness" is necessary for cooperation. Once again, there is a shift from a morality of constraint to a morality of cooperation. Piaget summarizes:

> In the first place, a lie is wrong because it is an object of punishment; if the punishment were removed, it would be allowed. Then a lie becomes something that is wrong in itself and would remain so even if the punishment were removed. Finally, a lie is wrong because it is in conflict with mutual trust and affection. Thus the consciousness of lying gradually becomes interiorized and the hypothesis may be hazarded that it does so under the influence of cooperation [p. 171].

Young children's "lies" are frequently spontaneous and not designed to deceive. Piaget writes:

> ... the tendency [in young children] to tell lies is a natural tendency, so spontaneous and universal that we can take it as an essential part of the child's egocentric thought. In the child, therefore, the problem of lies is the clash of the egocentric attitude with the moral constraint of the adult [p. 139].

The egocentric child frequently alters the truth according to his desires. Lying is viewed as "bad" by the young child *if it is punished* by adults. If, on the other hand, the child has some expectation that lying will go unpunished, he sees nothing morally wrong with lying.

PUNISHMENT AND JUSTICE

In Piaget's research on the development of children's concepts of justice, and more specifically on their concepts of punishment, two distinct kinds of punishment emerge. The concept of punishment Piaget observed in young children he calls *expiatory* punishment. Expiatory punishment is strong punishment, administered to children by parents or other adult authorities for breaking rules. The general reasoning children use to support the use of expiatory punishment as "just" is that "painful" punishment will deter further rule breaking. Expiatory punishment is *arbitrary* in character because it does not bear any relationship to the "crime." For example, a boy who did not clean up his room after being told to do so is punished by not being allowed to go to a movie. Or a child is sent on an important errand by the parent but does not carry out the request. The child is punished by not being allowed to play in the next school baseball game. In both cases the punishments are not related to the *content* of the rule broken. Had the first boy been deprived of the use of everything in his room he did not clean up, the punishment would not be arbitrary (regarding the content). Expiatory punishment is always handed out by authorities, involves constraint, and usually is arbitrary with respect to rules broken.

The second major punishment sanctioned by children Piaget calls *punishment by reciprocity*. Punishment by reciprocity assumes there is no need for "painful" punishment to gain adherence to rules. The person who breaks the rules must simply be made aware that breaking rules destroys the social relationship and the basic social contract of cooperation. This awareness, in itself, is believed to generate sufficient "grief" to restore and ensure cooperation. If material or social punishment is necessary, the punishment *is not arbitrary* (as is expiatory punishment). Punishment on the basis of reciprocity is *always* related in some way to the *content* of the rule broken. For example, the boy who did not clean up his room after being told to do so may be deprived of the objects (toys, clothes, books, etc.) he did not clean up. Or the child who did not perform a requested errand is denied similar help by his parents when the child requests it. These punishments are "natural consequences" of rule breaking and presumably help to point out to the child the consequences of his actions. While there can be a strong element of coercion in punishment by reciprocity, the emphasis is on persuasion and prevention rather than on punishment for its own sake. Punishment by reciprocity is guided by principles of cooperation and equality rather than adult authority and constraint.

Piaget investigated children's concepts of justice by telling them stories about children who did things they were not supposed to do, and asking them which forms of punishment were most appropriate or just. Here is one of the stories Piaget used:

> A little boy is playing in his room. His mother asks him to go and fetch some bread for dinner because there is none left in the house. But instead of going immediately the boy says that he can't be bothered, that he'll go in a minute, etc. An hour later he has not gone. Finally, dinner time comes, and there is no bread on the table. The father is not pleased and he

wonders which would be the fairest way of punishing the boy. He thinks of three punishments. The first would be to forbid the boy to go to the Roundabouts [fair] the next day.... The second punishment the father thought of was not to let the boy have any bread to eat. (There was a little bread left from the previous day.) ... The third punishment the father thinks of is to do to the boy the same thing as he had done. The father would say to him, "You wouldn't help your mother. Well I am not going to punish you, but the next time you ask me to do anything for you, I shall not do it, and you will see how annoying it is when people do not help each other." (The little boy thinks this would be all right, but a few days later his father would not help him reach a toy he could not get by himself. The father reminded him of his promise.) ... Which of these three punishments was the fairest? [p. 202].

Children between the ages of 6 and 12 years were told four stories and asked to judge which punishments were fairest and to give their *reasoning* for their judgments. Children were also asked to rate the punishments according to their severity. The responses children gave to the stories were classified as punishment by reciprocity or expiation, and the frequencies for different ages determined. Piaget found a distinct increase in children's preference for punishment by reciprocity with increase in age (see Table 3). Although some children at all ages recommended expiatory punishment as most appropriate, and some recommended punishment by reciprocity, a clear trend is evident. Younger children favored expiatory punishment; older children favored punishment by reciprocity.

TABLE 3

Ages	Percent of Children Preferring Punishment by Reciprocity
6-7	28
8-10	49
11-12	82

Ang (6) repeats story . . . correctly: "How should he be punished?—*Shut him up in a room.*—What will that do to him?—*He'd cry.*—Would that be fair?—*Yes.*" He is then told of the three possible punishments: "Which is the fairest?"—*I'd have not given him his toy.*—Why?—*He'd been naughty.*—Is that the best of the three punishments?—*Yes.*—Why?—*Because he was very fond of his toy.*—Is that the fairest?—*Yes.*" Thus it is not the principle of reciprocity that carries the day, it is the idea of the severest punishment [p. 211].

Zim (6): Zim does not think much of the last two punishments. The third "*is not hard.*—Why?—*On the little boy.*—Why is it not hard on him?—*It isn't much.*—The second is also "*not much.*" The fairest therefore is the first "*because he's not on the Roundabouts* [at the fair]" [p. 211].

Among younger children, the fairest punishment is the harshest; the punishments selected are arbitrary. It is clear that younger children believe in the need for severe punishment. As children develop, Piaget found that their concepts of justice change gradually. About half the children Piaget interviewed between the ages of 8 and 10 made judgments based on reciprocity and abandoned a criterion based on severity of punishment (expiatory punishment).

Buam (9): "*The last [punishment] is the best. Since the boy won't help, well his mother won't help him either.*—And which is the fairest of the other two punishments?—*Not to give him any bread, then he'd have nothing to eat at supper, because he wouldn't help his mother.*—And the first?—*That was the one he deserved least. He wouldn't have minded. He'd still have been able to play with his toys and he would have had bread in the evening*" [p. 215].

Nus (11) "*I'd have given him a smacking.*" The father thought of three punishments. (I tell them to him.) Which do you think is the fairest?—*Not to give him any help.*—Do you think it is fairer than smacking him?—*Fairer.*—Why?—(He hesitates.) . . . *Because it's doing about the same thing to him as he had done.*—And of the other two, which is the fairest?—*Not to let him have any bread.*—Why?—*Because he didn't fetch any*" [p. 216].

These interviews demonstrate that the older children Piaget interviewed view neither severe nor arbitrary punishment as the most appropriate. For these children, punishment based on reciprocity is more "just" than punishment based on expiation. The emphasis is clearly on punishment that "fits the crime," and helps the child to realize the social consequences of his actions. Older children's judgments as to which punishments are most appropriate seem to focus more on prevention and less on retaliation than do the judgments of younger children.

According to Piaget, it is difficult to develop a clear picture of the development of moral judgment that applies uniformly to all children. This is so for a number of reasons. Expiatory and reciprocal judgments are found at virtually all ages. Many adults function on the basis of expiatory punishment in preference to punishment based on reciprocity. In addition, Piaget suggests that concepts of justice are possibly influenced by *milieux* effects. That is, cultural or local conditions may encourage one form of reasoning over another. With these precautions in mind, Piaget asserted that children's concepts of justice evolve in a predictable manner. Young children typically make judgments that invoke expiatory punishment. Older children typically recognize the social significance of punishment; they favor punishment that is reciprocal in nature and "preventative" in design, and that communicates displeasure at the breaking of the social contract implicit in cooperation.

Piaget suggests that the concept of just punishment begins to be constructed by children only after a comprehension of rules emerges, generally around the age of 7 or 8. Concepts of rules, as noted, are developed as children interact with other children. All this occurs concurrent with a decline in intellectual egocentrism and an increased ability to see the viewpoint of others. In moral judgment we see an evolution from asocial judgments (expiatory punishment) to social judgments (reciprocity). Piaget writes:

> ... in every domain we have studied up till now, respect for the adult—or at any rate a certain way of respecting the adult— diminishes in favor of the relations of equality and reciprocity between children ... it is perfectly normal that in the domain of retribution [punishment] the effects of unilateral respect [egocentrism] should tend to diminish with age. ... What remains of the idea of retribution is the notion, not that one must compensate for the offence by a proportional suffering, but that one must make the offender realize, by means of measures appropriate to the fault itself, in what way he has broken the bond of solidarity. ...
>
> ... the idea of reciprocity, often taken at first as a sort of legalized vengeance or law of retaliation ... tends of itself towards a morality of forgiveness and understanding ... the time comes when the child realizes that there can be reciprocity

> only in well-doing. . . . The law of reciprocity implies certain positive obligations in virtue of its very form. And this is why the child, once he has admitted the principle of punishment by reciprocity in the sphere of justice, often comes to feel that any punitive element is unnecessary, even if it is "motivated," the essential thing being to make the offender realize that his action was wrong, in so far as it was contrary to the rules of cooperation [p.232].

Piaget concluded that three major periods exist in the development of children's concepts of justice. The first period lasts until age 7 or 8. In this period justice is subordinated to adult authority. The child accepts as just whatever adults (authorities) say is right. There is no distinction between the notion of just and unjust and the notion of duty and disobedience (Gruber and Voheche, 1977, p. 187). The child considers punishment to be the essence of justice.

The second period, between about 8 and 11 years, evolves concepts of cooperation. Reciprocity is viewed as the appropriate basis for punishment. A major emphasis is placed on "equality" of punishment, that laws are interpreted equally for all, and that all should receive the same (equal) punishment for the same "crime" regardless of the circumstance. Equality is viewed as more important than punishment. Expiatory punishment is no longer viewed as "just."

In the third period, usually beginning around age 11 or 12, reciprocity remains the basis for children's judgments about punishment, but children now consider intentions and situational variables (extenuating circumstances) when formulating judgments. Piaget calls this *equity*. Punishment need no longer be dispensed "equally" in a quantitative sense. For example, young children are held less liable than older children. At this level of development, judgments based on equity may be considered by the reader to be a more effective implementation of equality.

Summary

This overview of Piaget's major work on children's development of moral judgment outlines the general approach and results of Piaget's research in the 1930s. This is an introduction to a *portion* of Piaget's original research as presented in *The Moral Judgment of the Child*. The interested reader is encouraged to read Piaget's original work for a comprehensive account.

Piaget discovered that the reasoning underlying the moral judgments of children develops in a manner that parallels the development of general intelligence (as described by Piaget). Table 4 presents a summary of Piaget's findings regarding the development of children's concepts about *rules, accidents* (clumsiness), *lying*, and *justice*. Concepts can be seen to evolve (develop) in a pattern consistent with Piaget's description of intellectual development.

In the youngest children, those in the sensori-motor and early preoperational periods, rules and other moral values are not understood at all in an adult sense. Children reason that breaking rules is morally "bad" because it usually leads to punishment. Punishment becomes the criterion for right and wrong. Children's moral judgments prior to the end of the preoperational period of intellectual development (about age 7 or so) are constrained by their intellectual egocentrism. In an attempt to play the game of marbles with other children, they usually proceed without interacting with the other children. Behavior and reasoning during the early parts of the preoperational period are nonsocial.

Beginning with the development of concrete operations, children's social reasoning and interaction with others reflects a decline in intellectual egocentrism. Children begin to be able to consider situations from viewpoints other than their own. With respect to reciprocity, *equality* of

TABLE 4

Relationship Between Stages of Children's Cognitive Development and Stages of Development of Concepts of Rules, Accidents, Lying, and Justice

Cognitive Development	Rules	Accidents	Lying	Justice
Sensori-motor (0-2 years)	Motor Stage. Rules not observed			
Preoperational (2-7 years)	Egocentric stage. Games played in isolation. No cooperation or social interaction	Intentions not considered. Children do not take the view of others. Judgments based on quantitative effects of actions	Punishment the criterion for lie. No punishment = no lie. Lying is like being "naughty"	Submission to adult authority. Arbitrary, expiatory punishments considered just
Concrete operational (7-11 years)	Incipient cooperation. Rules are observed, though little agreement as to what the rules are	Intentions begin to be considered. Children begin to take the view of others	Lie = not true. Unpunished untruths are lies	Justice based on reciprocity. Equality more important than authority
Formal operations (after 11-12 years)	Codification of rules. Rules known to all. Agreement as to what the rules are. Rules can be changed by consensus. Rules of interest for their own sake		Intentions decide whether a false statement is not a lie. Truthfulness viewed as necessary for cooperation	Equality with equity. Reciprocity considers intent and circumstances

treatment becomes more important than punishment. Children begin to consider the intentions of others. There is a clear movement of the child's social and moral judgment from an egocentric punishment orientation to a more socialized view of justice based on cooperation. Laws and rules are no longer viewed as originating with adult authorities. Children are increasingly able to reason that laws are constructed by people and can be changed if there is agreement to do so. It becomes evident from children's thinking that the reasons why rules need to be upheld is because of the awareness that social groups cannot function without cooperation of their members.

WHAT PROMOTES MORAL REASONING?

If one accepts the premise that it is valuable to reason at the higher levels of moral development described by Piaget and Kohlberg, a relevant educational question is: How is the development of moral judgment maximized? This is in part the question: *How* (under what conditions) does moral judgment develop?

Moral judgment, or moral reasoning, can be classified as a form of *social knowledge*. As we noted in Chapter Two, social knowledge is knowledge that children *construct* out of their *interactions* with other people. Among young children, interactions with peers (rather than with adults) are the most significant interactions for activating development.

Children's initial moral concepts are shaped primarily by their interactions with those adults they view as authorities. Thus, these initial concepts reflect a morality of constraint. Children's early experiences are typically dominated by adult constraint. For the child, right or wrong is whatever the adult authority says it is. There is little in children's early experiences that encourages concepts of reciprocity and cooperation. Adult authority and preoperational *egocentrism* collectively work against the emergence of concepts based on cooperation. As long as the child is egocentric, there is little intellectual motivation for him to question his beliefs. For reasons such as these, Piaget argues that the concepts children eventually construct about justice, those based on reciprocity, cannot be built up directly from the child's early experience. Concepts of reciprocity cannot be constructed from concepts of authority.

> Authority as such cannot be the source of justice, because the development of justice presupposes autonomy. This does not mean ... that the adult plays no part in the development of justice. ... In so far as [the adult] practices reciprocity with the child and preaches by example rather than precept, he exercises here, as always, an enormous influence. But the most direct effect of adult ascendency is ... the feeling of duty, and there is a sort of contradiction between the submission demanded by duty [obeying *because of* authority] and the complete autonomy required by the development of justice. For resting as it does on equality and reciprocity, justice can only come into being by free consent. Adult authority, even if it acts in conformity with justice, has therefore the effect of weakening what constitutes the essence of justice [p. 319].

Piaget is not suggesting that children should not obey their parents. Nevertheless, what children learn from their experiences with adult authority cannot be the source of such concepts as reciprocity and cooperation. In fact, Piaget suggests that domination by authority in the early years may interfere with the development of moral reasoning. Adult authority provides the child with nothing he can use to *construct* a concept of reciprocity and nothing to help undo the child's egocentric view of the world. According to Piaget, the major force in the "overthrow" of authority as the only criterion for right and wrong, and the eventual decline of intellectual egocentrism, is usually the preoperational child's interaction with his peers. Out of these interactions children are forced to discover that other children have values different from their own, and that cooperation is a suitable basis for moral judgment. Justice is a concept each child constructs. The construction and the resulting reasoning cannot evolve from authority alone. Piaget writes:

> Thus, adult authority, although perhaps it constitutes a necessary moment in the moral evolution of the child, is not itself sufficient to create a sense of justice. This can develop only through progress made by cooperation and mutual respect—cooperation between children to begin with, and then between child and adult as the child approaches adolescence and comes, secretly at least, to consider himself as the adult's equal [pp. 319-320].

Although true social peer interactions begin in earnest during the preoperational period, it is not until about age 11 or 12 that most children begin to construct a concept of justice based on cooperation.

In the development of moral judgment the child changes from one who accepts authority as the basis of all values (morality of constraint) to one who constructs principles based on cooperation and reciprocity. In Piaget's view, the source of the merging concepts of cooperation is the child's interaction with peers (non-authorities). Authority in and of itself is not seen as a possible source of adult concepts of justice.

EDUCATIONAL IMPLICATIONS

Can parents and teachers do anything to help foster, or at least not interfere with, the development of moral judgment? Piaget has shown us how and under what conditions moral concepts are *constructed*. If the goals of education (at home and at school) include the development of sound moral judgment, cooperation, and other social values, and if we agree with Piaget's views, we can conclude that the authoritarian model for the relationship between children and adults is a poor one.[3] If children develop moral judgment, cooperation, and self-discipline in an authoritarian environment, it will have to be *in spite of*, rather than as a result of, their authoritarian relationship with adults. Piaget writes:

> It is ... absurd and even immoral to wish to impose upon the child a fully worked-out system of discipline when the social life of children themselves is sufficiently developed to give rise to a discipline infinitely nearer to the inner submission which is the mark of adult morality. It is idle ... to try and transform the child's mind from outside, when his own taste for active research and his desire for cooperation suffice to ensure a normal intellectual development. The adult must therefore be a collaborator and not a master, from this double point of view, moral and rational [p. 404].

Piaget recommends that schools foster active interactions between children, much in the way John Dewey (1963) described in the early 1900s. Authoritarian teachers need to discover ways to abandon their authoritarian role so that a major portion of their interaction with children can be as a collaborator and "equal." The development of cooperation by a child, as well as the development of self-discipline, can occur only in an environment that permits it.

---

[3] This is not an argument against adults exerting their authority over children when it is appropriate, but that children cannot be expected to develop advanced moral reasoning while authority remains the dominant moral force in their lives.

Piaget has not told us how to develop moral reasoning. What he has told us is how he believes moral reasoning develops. Like other knowledge, children *construct* moral knowledge and reasoning out of their *actions* in the environment. This tells us "how," not "how to." The leap from psychological theory to educational practice is a large one. Piaget recognized this. He writes:

> ... it is one thing to prove that cooperation in the play and spontaneous social life in children brings about certain moral effects, and another to establish the fact that this cooperation can be universally applied as a method of education [p. 406].

Neither Piaget, Kohlberg, nor any other psychologist or educator can provide the teacher or parent with a ready-made plan that will ensure children's development of moral reasoning. Common sense suggests that educational practice at home and in school should be *consistent with* what we know about children and their development. What follows are several guidelines consistent with Piaget's theory:

1. Teachers and parents can assume non-authoritarian relationships with children for at least some of their time together. Teachers can encourage children to resolve issues themselves.

2. When punishment of children is necessary, it can be based on reciprocity rather than expiation. For example, the child who refuses to clean up his room can be deprived of the things he does not clean up. The child who hits other children can be denied interaction with other children.

3. Teachers can foster a *pattern* of social interaction in their classrooms that encourages questioning and examining any issue children may raise. There is *intellectual* value in dealing with children's *spontaneous* intellectual in-

terests, and it is equally valuable to their moral development to deal with spontaneous moral questions.

4. Teachers can engage students, even at the pre-school level, in discussions of moral issues. As children listen to their peer's views, they can experience cognitive *disequilibration*, which can lead to re-organization of their concepts. Cognitive conflict is necessary for the restructuring of reasoning (development) to proceed.[4]

5. Schools and classrooms can be restructured to allow students greater participation in the *valid* aspects of the school-governing process. Although many "educators" would like to think otherwise, responsibility, cooperation, and self-discipline cannot be transmitted to children authoritatively. Such concepts must be constructed by children out of their own experiences. Teachers and parents are generally the ones who structure the social environment to which children adapt and from which they learn. It is questionable whether children can develop concepts of justice based on cooperation in an environment established on justice based on authority.

---

[4] A useful book containing suggestions for guidelines 4 and 5 is Hersh et al. (1977). While the book is long on Kohlberg and short on Piaget, it does present an excellent introduction to Kohlberg's work and addresses itself to educational application. I found the book to be generally compatible with the ideas expressed here.

Sensori-motor Preoperational Concrete Formal

Bibliography

Damon, W. "Conception of Positive Justice as Related to the Development of Logical Operations." *Child Development* 46 (1975): 301-312.

Dewey, J. *Education and Experience.* New York: Colliers, 1963.

Duckworth, E. "Either We're Too Early and They Can't Learn It, or We're Too Late and They Know It Already: The Dilemma of 'Applying Piaget,'" part II. *Genetic Epistemologist* 7, no. 4 (1978): 3-7.

Dupont, H. "Affective Development: Stage and Sequence (A Piagetian Interpretation)." In *Adolescent Development in Education,* edited by R. Mosher, Berkeley: McCutcheon, (in press).

Ebersole, M.; Kephart, N.; and Ebersole, J., *Steps to Achievement for the Slow Learner.* Columbus: Charles E. Merrill, 1968.

Elkind, D. "Children's Discovery of the Conservation of Mass, Weight, and Volume: Piaget's Replication Study II." *Journal of Genetic Psychology* 98 (1961): 219-227.

_____ . "Quality Conceptions in Junior and Senior High School Students." *Child Development* 32 (1961): 551-560.

_____ . "Quantity Conceptions in College Students." *Journal of Social Psychology* 57 (1962): 459-465.

_____ . "Egocentrism in Adolescence." *Child Development* 38 (1967): 1025-1034.

_____ . "Cognitive Structures and Adolescent Experience." *Adolescence* 2 (1967-1968): 427-434.

_____ . "Giant in the Nursery." *The New York Times Magazine* (May 26, 1968), 25.

_____ . Piagetian and Psychometric Conceptions of Intelligence." *Harvard Educational Review* 39 (1969): 319-337.

_____ . *Child Development and Education: A Piagetian Perspective.* New York: Oxford University Press, 1976.

_____ . "Is Piaget Passé in Elementary Education?" *Genetic Epistemologist* 7, no. 4 (1978): 1-2.

Erickson, E. *Childhood and Society.* New York: W. W. Norton, 1950.

Flavell, J. *The Developmental Psychology of Jean Piaget.* Princeton, N.J.: D. Van Nostrand, 1963.

Forman, G., and Kuschner, D. *The Child's Construction of Knowledge: Piaget for Teaching Children.* Belmont, Calif.: Brooks/Cole, 1977.

Freud, A. *The Ego and the Mechanisms of Defense.* New York: International Universities Press, 1946.

Gagné, R. M. "The Acquisition of Knowledge." *Psychological Review* 69 (1962): 355-365.

____. *The Conditions of Learning.* 3rd ed. New York: Holt, Rinehart and Winston, 1977.

Goldschmid, M. L. "Different Types of Conservation and Nonconservation and Their Relation to Age, Sex, I.Q., M. A., and Vocabulary." *Child Development* 38 (1967): 1229-1246.

Goodnow, J., and Bethon, G. "Piaget's Tasks: The Effects of Schooling and Intelligence." *Child Development* 37 (1966): 573-582.

Greenfield, P. M. "On Culture and Conservation." In *Studies in Cognitive Growth,* edited by J. Bruner et al. New York: Wiley, 1966.

Gruber, H., and Voneche, J., eds. *The Essential Piaget.* New York: Basic Books, 1977.

Gruen, G. E. "Experiences Affecting the Development of Number Conservation in Children." *Child Development* 36 (1965): 964-979.

Grzynkowicz, W. M., and Kephart, M., eds. *Learning Disabilities: Last Lectures of Newell C. Kephart.* Romeoville, Ill.: WGMK Publishers, 1975.

Hersh, R.; Paolitto, D.; and Reimer, J. *Promoting Moral Growth: From Piaget to Kohlberg.* New York: Longman, 1979.

Hooper, I. H. "Piagetian Research and Education." In *Logical Thinking in Children,* edited by I. E. Sigel and F. H. Hooper, pp. 423-434. New York: Holt, Rinehart and Winston, 1968.

Hunt, J. McV. *Intelligence and Experience.* New York: Ronald Press, 1961.

Inhelder, B., and Piaget, J. *The Growth of Logical Thinking from Childhood to Adolescence,* translated by Anne Parsons and Stanley Pilgram. New York: Basic Books, 1958.

____. *The Early Growth of Logic in the Child.* London: Routledge and Kegan Paul, 1964.

Kagan, J. "Emergent Themes in Human Development." *American Scientist* 64, no. 2 (March-April 1976): 186-196.

Kamii, C., and DeVries, R. *Physical Knowledge in Preschool Education: Implications of Piaget's Theory.* Englewood Cliffs, N.J., Prentice-Hall, 1978.

Kephart, N. C. *The Slow Learner in the Classroom*. Columbus: Charles E. Merrill, 1960.

———. "Perceptual-Motor Aspects of Learning Disabilities." *Exceptional Children* 31 (1964): 201-206.

Kohlberg, L. "The Development of Modes of Moral Thinking and Choice in the Years Two to Sixteen." Ph.D. dissertation, University of Chicago, 1958.

———. "Early Education: A Cognitive-Developmental View." *Child Development* 39 (1968): 1013-1063.

———. "The Montessori Approach to Cultural Deprivation. A Cognitive Development Interpretation and Some Research Findings." In *Preschool Education, Theory, Research, and Action*, edited by R. Hess and R. Bear. Chicago: Aldine, 1968.

———. "Stage and Sequence: The Cognitive-Developmental Approach to Socialization." In *Handbook of Socialization Theory and Research*, edited by D. Goslen, pp. 347-408. Chicago: Rand McNally, 1969.

———. "Moral Stages and Moralization: The Cognitive-Developmental Approach." In *Moral Development and Behavior: Theory, Research and Social Issues*, edited by T. Lickona. New York: Holt, Rinehart and Winston, 1976.

Kohlberg, L., and Mayer, R. "Development as the Aim of Education." *Harvard Educational Review* 42, no. 4 (November 1972): 449-496.

Kuhn, D. "Short-Term Longitudinal Evidence for the Sequentiality of Kohlberg's Early Stages of Moral Judgment." *Developmental Psychology* 12 (1976): 162-166.

Kuhn, D.; Langer, N.; Kohlberg, L.; and Hann, N. "The Development of Formal Operations in Logical and Moral Judgment." *Genetic Psychology Monograph* 95 (1977): 115.

L'Abate, L. "Frequency of Citation Study in Child Psychology Literature." *Child Development* 40 (1968): 87-92.

Mermelstein, E., and Schulman, L. "Lack of Formal Schooling and the Acquisition of Conservation." *Child Development* 38 (1967): 39-52.

Piaget, J. *The Language and Thought of the Child*. New York: Harcourt Brace Jovanovich, 1926.

———. *Judgment and Reasoning of the Child*. New York: Harcourt Brace Jovanovich, 1928.

———. *The Child's Conception of Physical Causality*. New York: Harcourt Brace Jovanovich, 1930.

____. *The Child's Conception of Number*. London: Humanities, 1952.

____. "Autobiography." In *History of Psychology in Autobiography,* edited by E. G. Boring et al., pp. 237-256. 4 vols. Worcester, Mass.: Clark University Press, 1952.

____. *The Origins of Intelligence in Children*. New York: International Universities Press, 1952.

____. *The Construction of Reality in the Child,* translated by Margaret Cook. New York: Basic Books, 1954.

____. "The Genetic Approach to the Psychology of Thought." *Journal of Educational Psychology* 52 (1961): 275-281.

____. *Play, Dreams and Imitation in Childhood*. New York: W. W. Norton, 1962.

____. *The Child's Conception of the World*. Paterson, N.J.: Littlefield, Adams, 1963.

____. *The Psychology of Intelligence*. Paterson, N.J.: Littlefield, Adams, 1963.

____. "Three Lectures." In *Piaget Rediscovered,* edited by R. E. Ripple and U. N. Rockcastle. Ithaca, N.Y.: Cornell University Press, 1964.

____. *The Moral Judgment of the Child*. New York: Free Press, 1965.

____. *Six Psychological Studies*. New York: Vintage Books, 1967.

____. *The Mechanisms of Perception*. New York: Basic Books, 1969.

____. *Genetic Epistemology*. New York: Columbia University Press, 1970.

____. *Science of Education and the Psychology of the Child*. New York: Viking Press, 1970.

Piaget, J., and Inhelder, B. *The Child's Conception of Space*. London: Routledge and Kegan Paul, 1956.

____. *The Psychology of the Child,* translated by Helen Weaver. New York: Basic Books, 1969.

Piaget, J.; Inhelder, B.; and Szeminska, A. *The Child's Conception of Geometry*. New York: Basic Books, 1960.

Pinard, A., and Laurendeau, M. "A Scale of Mental Development Based on the Theory of Piaget: Description of a Project." *Journal of Research in Science Teaching* 2 (1964): 253-260.

Rosenthal, R., and Jacobson, L. *Pygmalion in the Classroom*. New York: Holt, Rinehart and Winston, 1968.

Selman, R. L. "The Relation of Role-Taking to the Development of Moral Judgment in Children." *Child Development* 42 (1971): 59-91.

Selman, R. L. "Social-Cognitive Understanding: A Guide to Educational and Clinical Practice." In *Moral Development and Behavior: Theory, Research and Social Issues*, edited by T. Lickona, New York: Holt, Rinehart and Winston, 1976.

Sigel, I. E. "The Attainment of Concepts." In *Review of Child Development Research,* edited by M. L. Hoffman and L. V. Hoffman, vol. 1, pp. 209-248. New York: Russell Sage Foundation, 1964.

Sigel, I. E., and Hooper, F. H. *Logical Thinking in Children: Research Based on Piaget's Theory*. New York: Holt, Rinehart and Winston, 1968.

Smedslund, J. "The Acquisition of Conservation of Substance and Weight in Children." In *Readings in Child Development and Behavior,* edited by G. Stendler. New York: Harcourt Brace Jovanvich, 1964.

Uzgiris, I. "Situational Generality of Conservation." In *Logical Thinking in Children*, edited by I. E. Sigel and F. H. Hooper, pp. 40-52. New York: Holt, Rinehart and Winston, 1968.

Wadsworth, B. "The Effect of Peer Group Social Interaction on the Conservation of Number Learning in Kindergarten Children." Ed.D. dissertation, State University of New York at Albany, 1968.

_____. *Piaget for the Classroom Teacher*. New York: Longman, 1978.

_____. "Piaget's Concept of Adaptation and Its Value to Educators." In *Piagetian Theory and the Helping Professions* (Eighth Annual Conference Proceedings). Los Angeles: University of Southern California, (in press).

Wadsworth, B., and Cody, J. "Frequency of Citation in *Child Development* in 1974." Manuscript, Mount Holyoke College, n.d.

Wallach, L., Wall, J., and Anderson, L. "Number Conservation: The Roles of Reversibility, Addition, Subtraction, and Misleading Perceptual Cues." *Child Development* 38 (1967): 425-442.

Wohlwill, J., and Lowe, R. "Experimental Analysis of the Development of Conservation of Number." *Child Development* 33 (1962): 153-168.

Zimiles, H. "The Development of Differentiation and Conservation of Number." *Monograph Society for Research in Child Development* 31 (1966).

Index

187